THE URGENCY
OF NOW

The Association of Community College Trustees and Rowman & Littlefield Publishers

The Futures Series on Community Colleges

Sponsored by the Association of Community College Trustees and Rowman & Littlefield Publishers, *The Futures Series on Community Colleges* is designed to produce and deliver books that strike to the heart of issues that will shape the future of community colleges. *Futures* books examine emerging structures, systems, and business models, and stretch prevailing assumptions about leadership and management by reaching beyond the limits of convention and tradition.

Topics addressed in the *Series* are those that are vital to community colleges, but have yet to receive meaningful attention in literature, research, and analysis. *Futures* books are written by scholars and practitioners who deliver a unique perspective on a topic or issue—a president or higher education consultant bringing expert and practical understanding to a topic, a policy analyst breaking down a complex problem into component parts, an academic or think tank scholar conducting incisive research, or a researcher and a practitioner working together to examine an issue through different lenses.

Futures books are developed on the premise that disruptive innovation and industry transformation are, and will be, an ongoing challenge. Gradual improvement is, understandably, a natural preference of leaders. It will not be enough, however, to position our colleges for the future. The future will be about transformation and, to perform optimally, our colleges will need to become capable of large-scale change. As leaders come face-to-face with digital forces and rapidly changing social, economic, and public policy conditions, they will have no choice but to get ahead of change or relinquish market position to competitors. *Futures* books are a vehicle through which leaders can learn about and prepare for what's ahead. Whether it's through analysis of what big data will mean in the next generation of colleges, or which business models will become the new normal, *Futures* books are a resource for practitioners who realize that the ideas of out-of-the-box thinkers and the innovative practices of high-performing organizations can be invaluable for answering big questions and solving complex problems.

Richard L. Alfred, Series Co-Editor
Emeritus Professor of Higher Education
University of Michigan

Debbie Sydow, Series Co-Editor
President
Richard Bland College of the College of William and Mary

Forthcoming Books in
The Futures Series on Community Colleges

Financing America's Community Colleges: Where We Are, Where We're Going
By Richard Romano and James Palmer
Grounded in an economic perspective, *Financing America's Community Colleges* helps college leaders make sense of the challenges they face in securing and managing the resources needed to carry out the community college mission. Finance has perpetually been an Achilles' heel for leaders at all levels of management. With the premise that leaders are better at winning battles they know something about, this book equips leaders with an understanding of the fundamentals and the complexities of community college finance. It tackles current and emerging issues with insight that is analytic and prophetic—a must-read for current and prospective leaders.

Unrelenting Change, Disruptive Innovation, and Risk: Forging the Next Generation of Community Colleges
By Daniel J. Phelan
In this book, thirty-five-year veteran Dan Phelan shares key insights from his personal and professional journey as a transformational, entrepreneurial community college leader. The book's wisdom and insights are amplified by observations gleaned from interviews and visits with dozens of leading practitioners. Drawing upon his sailing experiences, Phelan argues that leaders should stop playing it safe in the harbor because the real gains driving institutional and student success are found in uncharted waters. *Unrelenting Change, Disruptive Innovation, and Risk* dares community college leaders to innovate and provides them with a tool kit for understanding changing conditions, assessing risk, and successfully navigating change.

The Urgency of Now: Equity and Excellence
By Marcus M. Kolb, Samuel D. Cargile, et al.
The Urgency of Now asserts that in addition to being granted access to the community college, all twenty-first-century students need uncompromised support to succeed. Success means demonstrating relevant learning for transfer and employment and timely completion of credentials. Looking to the future, the authors contend that community colleges, both because of their past successes and future challenges, are at the epicenter for determining the essential ingredients of a new student-centered system that guarantees equity and excellence.

The Completion Agenda in Community Colleges: What It Is, Why It Matters, and Where It's Going
By Chris Baldwin

Community colleges in many states are facing intensifying pressure from policy makers for improved student outcomes overtly manifested in aggressive performance-based funding formulas. In this book, Chris Baldwin asks and answers an overarching question: Are community colleges, government agencies, foundations, and other entities aware of the unintended consequences of actions related to the completion agenda? The book explores the potential benefit of increased educational attainment and credentials versus the possible sacrifice of quality and the labor market value of the credentials awarded.

Institutional Analytics: Building a Culture of Evidence
By Karen Stout

Institutional Analytics paints a clear picture of the challenges involved in cultural change and building a team capable of using analytics to gain a competitive advantage for the future. Revealing that community colleges pretend to be more data driven than they actually are, Stout challenges leadership teams to set clear goals, define what success looks like, and ask the right questions to get there. By adopting new tools, abandoning legacy systems and relationships, and boldly adopting open source solutions, colleges can turn large quantities of data into business intelligence that drives transformation.

Previously Published Books in
The Series on Community Colleges

Minding the Dream: The Process and Practice of the American Community College, Second Edition
By Gail O. Mellow and Cynthia M. Heelan

First in the World: Community Colleges and America's Future
By J. Noah Brown

Community College Student Success: From Boardrooms to Classrooms
By Banessa Smith Morest

Re-visioning Community Colleges
By Debbie Sydow and Richard Alfred

Community Colleges on the Horizon: Challenge, Choice, or Abundance
By Richard Alfred, Christopher Shults, Ozan Jaquette, and Shelley Strickland

THE URGENCY OF NOW

Equity and Excellence

**Marcus M. Kolb,
Samuel D. Cargile,
Jason Wood,
Nassim Ebrahimi,
Lynn E. Priddy, and
Laurie Dodge**

**with Richard L. Alfred and
Debbie L. Sydow**

ASSOCIATION OF
COMMUNITY COLLEGE TRUSTEES

ROWMAN & LITTLEFIELD
Lanham • Boulder • New York • London

Published by Rowman & Littlefield
A wholly owned subsidiary of The Rowman & Littlefield Publishing Group, Inc.
4501 Forbes Boulevard, Suite 200, Lanham, Maryland 20706
www.rowman.com

Unit A, Whitacre Mews, 26-34 Stannary Street, London SE11 4AB

British Library Cataloguing in Publication Information Available

Library of Congress Cataloging-in-Publication Data Available

ISBN 978-1-4758-1450-7 (cloth : alk. paper)
ISBN 978-1-4758-1451-4 (pbk. : alk. paper)
ISBN 978-1-4758-1452-1 (electronic)

∞™ The paper used in this publication meets the minimum requirements of American National Standard for Information Sciences—Permanence of Paper for Printed Library Materials, ANSI/NISO Z39.48-1992.

Printed in the United States of America

CONTENTS

FOREWORD

There can no longer be any question that the work community colleges do is integral to our national future. Over the last decade, the sector has been the subject of unprecedented research, thoughtful critique, and, occasionally, brutally honest criticism.

Spurred largely by the early and ongoing interest and support of Lumina Foundation and other philanthropic leaders, community colleges have become more transparent, more data-driven, and more focused on student success than at any time in their 114-year history. Their national associations and institutional leaders have embraced the challenge of what can only be seen as historic and fundamental transformation.

What the editors and authors of *The Urgency of Now: Equity and Excellence* now overlay on this complex equation is an overriding urgency—what they aptly term the "urgency of now."

For those of us who have made community colleges our life's work, it is an urgency that is at once inspiring, challenging, and, in some instances, deeply concerning.

Expectations of markedly improved student outcomes and institutional accountability have been steadily rising for the nation's community colleges. Policy makers call for higher levels of performance and productivity, increasingly as a condition for funding. Employers expect closer alignment of student learning with the needs of the workplace. Most importantly, for more than thirteen million students, the hope of closing achievement gaps and achieving economic parity rests squarely on our collective shoulders.

Any realistic hope of meeting those expectations will require bold and wholesale change. The key to that change, as Dr. Sam Cargile astutely observes in his introduction to the book, is that ". . . higher education become a student-centered system," with community colleges at "the epicenter of determining what the essential ingredients" of such a system should be.

The critical importance of student-centric learning, a prevailing emphasis throughout this book, has gained greater traction among community colleges than arguably any other sector of higher education. We would be remiss not to acknowledge the early scholarship of Drs. Robert Barr and John Tagg, and the extensive advocacy of leaders such as Dr. Terry O'Banion who framed and worked to advance the "learning college" concept almost two decades ago.

But despite what we *know* about how students learn best, says Dr. Jason Wood (chapter 1), it is what we *do* that matters most. Historically, Woods says, higher education has "focused on teaching with faculty as the center rather than students."

A recent white paper from the American Council on Education's Presidential Innovation Lab supports that opinion, noting that changes in faculty roles "[h]ave almost never been an intentional effort to redesign faculty roles in a way that is focused on student learning or serving institutional missions."

Wood asserts that a primarily faculty focus is antithetical to optimum student learning. Further, it is measurable student learning that serves as a proxy for quality in education—the "excellence" of the book's title. Further exacerbating the problem, he says, is our entrenched reliance on mechanisms such as the Carnegie unit as a measure of quality versus a measure of time. Despite its long-standing and pervasive use in higher education, the credit hour tells us virtually nothing about student learning, Wood says.

Having posited student learning as a proxy for quality and the key to greater student success in every aspect of the learning enterprise, succeeding chapters of the book explore practical—sometimes provocative—

ways to reach the high bar of equity with excellence. Dr. Lynn Priddy, who spent fourteen years with the Higher Learning Commission of the North Central Association of Colleges and Schools, the nation's largest regional accreditor, touches on the decade-long prominence of what is commonly termed the "completion agenda" (chapter 2).

In her analysis, Priddy examines the intertwining relationships between learning, persistence, and completion from the standpoint of accreditation and describes a new, transformative role for accreditors—from proctors of compliance to "catalysts for the evolution to student centeredness."

Authors Laurie Dodge and Nassim Ebrahimi (chapters 3 and 4) bring a rich and informed context to the book's examination of competency-based learning and integrated assessment. Dr. Dodge currently chairs the Competency-Based Education Network and offers insight into the network's efforts to advance the design and scaling of degree programs based not on "seat time" but on cumulative learning experiences from myriad sources.

Her analysis offers not only a concise history of competency-based education but also advice on designing such a program. Dr. Ebrahimi is nationally recognized for her expertise in developing systemized assessments at multiple levels. Both provide examples, case studies, and useful guidance to help college leaders answer questions of whether, when, and how to implement change strategies.

Having made the critical importance of student-centered learning the central premise of the book, it is fitting that Dr. Marcus Kolb concludes with a discussion of faculty engagement (chapter 5), for it is here that transformation will either succeed or flounder.

As the acknowledged frontline of learning, faculty represent what a 2010 study from the Center of Community College Student Engagement asserted is "the heart of student success." Kolb presents a cogent analysis of the barriers and opportunities inherent in faculty engagement, from perceived threats to the instructor's professional identity and classroom control to the importance of effective messaging. In essence, he presents a guideline for evolving faculty attitudes "from *my* work to *my* institution."

The need to engage faculty—both full-time and adjunct—in integrated leadership roles across the institution resonates with strategies presented in the American Association of Community Colleges' *Empowering Community Colleges to Build the Nation's Future* report, the implementation guide relating to AACC's 21st Century Initiative.

Other recommendations presented in *The Urgency of Now* also amplify the thrust of AACC's ongoing work and that of the many individuals and organizations committed to transforming our institutions.

Early in *The Urgency of Now* narrative, Jason Wood succinctly captures the enormity of reinventing the learning experience with students' needs at the center. "Higher education, as it has historically been configured, simply does not work for most of the students who need it most."

Our challenge is daunting and stark. But the tremendous commitment already in evidence on the nation's community college campuses and the progress these "incubators of innovation" have made in a relatively short period of time inspire us and spur us on. It is the *urgency* of our shared task that the authors of *The Urgency of Now* drive home in this compelling new work.

—Dr. Walter G. Bumphus,
President, American Association of Community Colleges

ACKNOWLEDGMENTS

The concept of "team" takes on a great deal of meaning when writing a book. Besides a great group of colleagues as authors, many others contribute their time, talent, and encouragement. We would be remiss in not acknowledging series editors Dr. Debbie Sydow and Dr. Richard Alfred. They were diligent in teaching us what we needed to know, keeping us on time, and always standing ready to answer our questions. They made this process much, much easier.

We extend thanks to Terri Steward at Lumina Foundation. Her assistance in scheduling meetings and conference calls kept things moving in an orderly manner.

Writing this book also reminds us that while we have much to do to make our community colleges—indeed, all of higher education—a better place for all students, there are many talented people already hard at work at designing and implementing the transformations we discuss and that are so desperately needed. We know that change will not be inhibited by a lack of good ideas or resources. It can only be squashed by a lack of desire to change. And we simply cannot afford to wait any longer to become a student-centered, learning-driven enterprise. Our students need this from us now, more than ever.

Samuel Cargile: This book simply would not have been possible without the thought-provoking leadership of series editors Richard Alfred and Debbie Sydow. They challenged and encouraged at just the right moments. As the sole contributor who is not based at an institution, it was a privilege to work with, and learn from, my five colleagues who are, Laurie Dodge, Nassim Ebrahimi, Marcus Kolb, Lynn Priddy, and Jason Wood. I have such great respect for their unwavering dedication to ensuring that many more students of color and first-generation students succeed in attaining their goals in the twenty-first century. Finally, special appreciation to Dr. Frankie Felder at Clemson University, who on more occasions than I can count was an invaluable sounding board.

Laurie Dodge: Thank you to my husband, John Dodge, who is my rock and my wings and the best dance partner imaginable.

Nassim Ebrahimi: In my career, I've been fortunate to work with amazingly talented leaders in higher education. To my co-authors, thank you for your guidance and support. I've learned so much from your passion, dedication, and expertise. To my mentor and friend, Dr. Jean M. Runyon, who inspires me each and every day to reflect, grow, and make a lasting difference in the lives of students, thank you. To my friends and colleagues, thank you for supporting me on this journey. Most importantly, to Kian, Donya, Reza, Mitra, mom, and dad, without you I would not be who I am today. You mean the world to me!

Marcus Kolb: Turns out you learn far more than you share when working with a talented group of colleagues. Thank you to my co-authors. I am grateful to my friends and colleagues at the Lumina Foundation and Ivy Tech for the support and encouragement to engage in and finish this work. Special thanks to Dr. Cargile for raising the specter of writing this and then helping to lead us all through it. Thanks to my wife, Freedom, and my three daughters, Emersen, Sullivan, and Monroe, for allowing Dad time to read, write, and edit on weekend mornings and a couple of late nights. It always begins and ends with the four of you.

Lynn Priddy: The opportunity to capture provocative ideas from conversations with colleagues on the state of learning, higher education, and accreditation has been inspiring and energizing. Writing a chapter and book collaboratively creates a community that can make a difference. Great thanks is owed to the interviewees for their honesty and willingness to allow me to print their real voices versus careful quotes. My hope is that the book provokes transformation over tweaking, restoration of learning and aspiration as central to quality, and pursuit of learning over both completion and compliance. Special appreciation goes to Roberta Teahen and Monica Manning for refusing to let the writing rest.

Jason Wood: Thank you to my professional mentors, Dr. Jo Anne McFarland, Dr. Rob Frost, and Dr. Gayle Lawn-Day, for helping me to learn through thick and thin. Thank you to the best colleagues ever—Martha Davey and Michelle Rosales. Mom and Dad, thanks for more than everything. A special thank you to Kathryn for her love, faith, and patience as we raise our six wonderful daughters, Natalie, Melanie, Heidi, Amy, Brynlee, and Sadie. Here's to hoping higher education takes bold steps forward in time for my daughters to reap the benefits.

INTRODUCTION

The Urgency of Now—Equity and Excellence
Samuel D. Cargile

The U.S. Supreme Court decision in *Fisher v. the University of Texas* revived a long-standing debate in higher education admissions about the trade-offs between equity and excellence.[1]

The time has long since passed for such debates. The nation must have both. Lumina Foundation believes that closing the attainment gap between whites and racial minority groups that have historically been underserved by higher education because of their race (African Americans, American Indians, and Hispanic Americans) is essential to achieving what they believe should be the nation's goal of 60 percent of Americans possessing high-quality postsecondary degrees and credentials by 2025. They also believe that Goal 2025 is the best pathway for remaining economically competitive in a global society and ensuring a vibrant national democracy in which all citizens have an opportunity to equally participate.[2]

Ironically, the equity versus excellence debate comes at the same time when the rapidly progressing evolution of higher education in the United States has forced a reconception of the meaning of quality degrees and credentials, and a reconsideration of definitions of student learning outcomes. Where once it was acceptable to define credentials by credit hours and to define quality by the qualifications of entering students or the bona fide occupational qualifications of faculty, stakeholders have lost faith in these measures, and greater accountability is evolving as a result.

Consequently, change is afoot to define postsecondary degrees and credentials by what students know and are able to do at the conclusion of courses and programs of study, regardless of sources of learning or time spent in developing and practicing skills and knowledge. The essence of what students know and the ability that students demonstrate in applying what they know has become the true definition of quality in higher education and the workforce for the foreseeable future.

As President Eduardo Padron of Miami Dade College noted, community colleges are on the frontline of "battling inequality" while also being charged with providing high-quality instruction that leads to meaningful degrees, credentials, and employment.[3]

A WAY FORWARD

Since its inception in 2000, Lumina Foundation has focused exclusively on increasing access and success in higher education for all students, with the bulk of the work centered on community colleges. Through support for efforts like the Community College Survey of Student Engagement, Achieving the Dream, Credit When It's Due, Win-Win, the Degree Qualifications Profile and Tuning USA, and the Competency-Based Education Network, among many others, the work has evolved from merely increasing completion rates to improving and assuring the quality of the learning outcomes that postsecondary degrees and credentials represent.

In 2012, the Foundation issued a clarion call to increase the percentage of Americans with high-quality postsecondary degrees and credentials from the long-standing 39 percent to 60 percent by the year 2025. Goal 2025, as it came to be known, was a direct result of what was learned from the aforementioned efforts.

Equity also was integral to Goal 2025. Based on data in its *Stronger Nation* reports, the Foundation concluded that unless significant progress is made to close gaps in attainment for African Americans, American Indians, and Hispanic Americans, Goal 2025 simply is not attainable. The picture is further exacerbated because many of the students in these groups (compared to white students) are from lower-income situations and are the first in their families to attend college, which increase the odds of not attaining a postsecondary degree or credential without effective interventions at the institutional level.[4]

Two recent reports further underscore the importance of inextricably linking equity with learning and innovation.

In *Separate and Unequal: How Higher Education Reinforces the Intergenerational Reproduction of White Privilege*, Anthony Carnevale and Jeff Strohl reported that "White students are increasingly concentrated . . . in the nation's 468 most well-funded, selective four-year colleges and universities while African-American and Hispanic students are more and more concentrated in the 3,250 least-well funded, open access, two- and four-year colleges."[5]

They concluded that this racial and ethnic divide matters because resources matter. "Greater postsecondary resources and completion rates (most selective colleges 82 percent, compared to 49 percent for open-admission colleges and two-year colleges) for white students concentrated in the 468 most selective colleges confer substantial labor market advantages, including more than \$2 million per student in higher lifetime earnings, and access to professional and managerial elite jobs, as well as careers that bring personal and social empowerment."[6]

In *Bridging the Higher Education Divide: Strengthening Community Colleges and Restoring the American Dream*, the Century Foundation Task Force on Preventing Community Colleges from Becoming Separate and Unequal made two recommendations—in particular—that suggest a way forward for overcoming the growing racial and economic divide between two- and four-year colleges described by Carnevale and Strohl, and pertain both to reaching Goal 2025 as well as the thrust of *The Urgency of Now: Equity and Excellence*.

The first recommendation calls for innovations in accountability and funding. The Task Force proposed adoption of state and federal adequacy-based funding in higher education similar to that used in K-12, combined with considerations of outcomes. Specifically, ". . . tying new accountability plans to greater funding for institutions serving those students with the greatest needs . . . coupled with consideration of student outcomes, such as job placements, degrees earned, transfers to four-year institutions."[7]

The second recommendation calls for innovations in governance to reduce economic and racial stratification by strengthening the connections between community colleges and four-year institutions. One particularly promising and timely example cited is blending elements of two- and four-year colleges in one setting. In this example, degree programs would be based on student learning outcomes and competencies, rather than credit hours.[8]

STUDENTS AT THE CENTER

Looking toward the future, it is critical that higher education become a student-centered system. Not only must access be ensured for all of today's twenty-first-century students, but these students must also receive the support they need to succeed. Success means earning credentials in a timely way and demonstrating relevant learning with regard to further education and employment.

The major premise of *The Urgency of Now: Equity and Excellence* is that community colleges, both by their past successes and future challenges, are at the epicenter for determining what the essential ingredients of such a student-centered system should be, and how this student-centered system can successfully be used by both two- and four-year institutions.

NOTES

1. *Fisher v. University of Texas*, 113 S. Ct. 2411, at 2420 (2013).

2. Jamie Merisotis, president/CEO Lumina Foundation, "The Urgency of Now: Beyond Fisher" (New York: Huffington Post, July 26, 2013); *A Stronger Nation through Higher Education* (Indianapolis: Lumina Foundation, April 2014).

3. Eduardo Padron, "Community Colleges Are on the Front Lines Battling Inequality" (New York: Al Jazeera America, December 3, 2013).

4. Xianglei Chen, "First Generation Students in Postsecondary Education: A Look at Their College Transcripts" (Washington, D.C.: National Center for Educational Statistics, 2005; U.S. Census Bureau, Current Population Survey, 2009).

5. Anthony P. Carnevale and Jeff Strohl, *Separate and Unequal: How Higher Education Reinforces the Intergenerational Reproduction of White Racial Privilege* (Washington, D.C.: The Georgetown University Center on Education and the Workforce, 2013), 16–20.

6. Anthony P. Carnevale, Stephen J. Rose, and Ban Cheah, *The College Payoff* (Washington, D.C.: The Georgetown University Center on Education and the Workforce, 2011), 3–4.

7. The Report of The Century Foundation Task Force on Preventing Community Colleges from Becoming Separate and Unequal, *Bridging the Higher Education Divide: Strengthening Community Colleges and Restoring the American Dream* (New York: The Century Foundation Press, 2013), 7–8.

8. Ibid., 7–8.

MAKING THE CASE

Jason Wood

The Urgency of Now is that there is little time left for community colleges to become twenty-first-century, student-centered institutions. They must find new ways not only to clearly articulate what their students know and how well they can apply that knowledge in meaningful and relevant situations, but also to make it happen in the teaching and learning process.

Community colleges, long the incubators of innovation in higher education and servants to the widest swath of students, again must be in the forefront of leading the way to productive change in student learning outcomes. A major premise of this book is that this change must be accelerated while ensuring both high-quality teaching and learning.

Higher education, as it has historically been configured, simply does not work for most of the students who need it the most. Twenty years ago, Barr and Tag made a case for moving from a teaching to a learning paradigm in higher education. They argued that the shift from teaching to learning occurs when colleges and universities realize that "teaching" is a means to an end and not an end in and of itself. They also noted that the process of changing from a teaching to a learning organization will not happen instantaneously. Rather, it will occur through "a process of gradual modification and experimentation."[1]

WHY THE RUSH?

There is an urgency to transform community colleges, through innovation and excellence, from primarily teaching institutions into truly student-centered learning communities. Despite the progress in defining and assessing student learning, in creating new student-focused pathways through higher education, and in designing new curricula and pedagogy for better learning, community colleges and all of higher education continue to struggle with applying what we know works for students. As Kuh and Ikenberry note, we draw blood from the student in the form of assessment of learning and often fail to review the blood test results, student learning, and chart a course of treatment.[2]

Accessible and Affordable

The idea of higher education being accessible and affordable for all was an innovation that differentiated community colleges from the long-standing notion that higher education is only for a select few individuals. It is now time for another transformative innovation to propel community colleges forward yet again. The urgency is for community colleges to maintain their history of wide access while also ensuring that high-quality student learning outcomes are at the forefront of its mission as well.

In fact, the very notion of non-traditional students (i.e., low-income, people of color, full-time workers, single parents, etc.) enrolling in community colleges because of lower costs or geographic convenience is precisely the reason a major emphasis must be placed on quality learning at a reasonable price. The truth is that these students simply have almost no other options that will help them to achieve their education and career goals.

Demographics

Community colleges, as flexible and adaptive institutions that take pride in being responsive to students, must also take the lead in transitioning to a student-focused model of higher education. Indeed, they have long been recognized as teaching institutions with faculty both teaching and providing significant student support as a unique form of service, creativity, and scholarship, in contrast to more classic forms of research and publication at their four-year counterparts.

They also have taken great care to ensure that their services are, first and foremost, focused on all types of learners through open access to all in their immediately surrounding community.[3]

The demographics of students participating in higher education have changed. Community colleges are best positioned to lead innovations that affect learning for a more diverse student body than ever before. In fact, the student demographic of community colleges is perhaps the most diverse of any education sector. The American Association of Community Colleges reports that half of the students enrolled in community colleges do not identify themselves as white.[4]

With students of all ages, varying educational abilities, unique goals, and differing socioeconomic statuses, community colleges reflect the communities they serve and must play the pivotal role in reducing the postsecondary degree and credential attainment gap between the racial groups mentioned later in this book.

Workforce Needs and Trends

Community colleges take great pride in being nimble and flexible in developing curricula that can be adapted to meet emerging workforce needs and trends. Close connections with workforce partners and potential employers of graduates afford community colleges an opportunity for students to immediately demonstrate their abilities and apply the learning from the classroom in a real setting.

The *shift* to institutions focused on student learning outcomes will facilitate even greater opportunities for closer relationships with business and industry as employers realize the benefits of pre-hire training programs that develop key competencies and proficiencies in students' abilities.

For example, two industries at the forefront of national and international issues are health care and technology. The health-care and technology worlds are increasingly intertwined and constantly evolving. Degree options that are customizable, relevant, and rigorous could conceivably accommodate the workforce demand for employees who have been prepared in both disciplines.

To extend the example, let's take a brief look at Central Wyoming College (CWC). A student who was employed by a local hospital recognized the need for additional training in order to be more valuable to her employer. The only problem was the fact that her employer needed skills in disparate areas: technology and medical coding. By working with a dean at CWC and her employer, a customized road map to a relevant degree in information technology and medical coding and billing emerged.

Moreover, before completing her degree, the student was promoted primarily due to the skills and proficiencies she acquired in the classroom. After graduation, she was promoted again. Both the student and employer later reported that the skills gained in the flexible academic program made it possible for both promotions, representing the best of what community colleges can and should be doing for twenty-first-century students.

CLOSING THE ATTAINMENT GAP

For many, degree or credential attainment is *the* major challenge to the open-access mission that is inherently characteristic of most community colleges.[5] While the emphasis on attainment is timely and certainly provides a challenge to the access mission of community colleges, less attention has been paid to the issue of quality. In higher education, the best proxy for quality should be student learning.

Student Learning and Faculty Teaching

Another premise of this book is that the quality of student learning also should be the focus for closing the achievement gap, as quality learning promotes success. Courses, programs of study, credentials, and degrees require clear articulation and alignment of learning outcomes for development of quality assessments, assurance of relevance in the workplace and further education, and marketing of programs to students and other stakeholders.

New tools, like the Degree Qualifications Profile, Moxilla Badges, direct assessment as part of competency-based education, the Adult Learners

Guide, and the VALUE Rubrics, support the notion of the transition from teaching to learning, suggesting a growing focus on competencies in the community college classroom.[6] Competencies are being considered as a new currency in learning. The federal government is also experimenting with ways for financial aid to be disbursed to students in competency-based programs rather than credit-based programs.[7]

However, historically, higher education has focused on teaching with faculty as the center rather than students. An emphasis on teaching and the faculty encompasses every aspect of academic, operational, and administrative practices. For example, the Carnegie unit for credit hours has been the primary instrument used to measure the time needed for teaching, to calculate the cost of education for tuition purposes, and to develop a schedule of courses within a block of time. As Latinen reported, "The problem is that over the years, the credit hour's use has expanded beyond measures of time to serve as a proxy for learning."[8]

The Carnegie unit says nothing about learning and, in fact, casts the work of the institution in terms of faculty time and not in terms of student learning and success. And while the focus on teaching has served some students well—primarily those who would be successful in higher education no matter the format—many others fall through the cracks and do not complete a degree, rack up debt, or, even if successful, fail to find employment in their field of study. In 2015, the Department of Education reported that nationally the community college graduation rate is only 31 percent.[9] The nation can—and must—do much better!

Challenge Meets Opportunity

The Obama administration has made strengthening community colleges a priority.[10] The recent proposal to make community college tuition-free has sparked a national conversation that shines an important light on closing the attainment gap.

On one hand, community colleges provide affordable access to millions of students, helping them to successfully transfer to a university or prepare for a specific career. On the other hand, many community colleges will have to answer for poor performance on progression, performance, and—ultimately—graduation rates. Regardless, the president's proposal is a great opportunity for community colleges. It is an opportunity to be front and center in the national debate on the value of higher education by demonstrating through both policy and practice that community colleges play a unique role in producing a *scaled* educated workforce and citizenry.

Another aspect of the administration's advocacy includes promoting industry and college partnerships to foster career readiness. Community colleges have an opportunity to remain at the forefront of these partnerships, especially as the pace at which they are changing is accelerating. Regulatory agencies, state and national lawmakers, and private and public funding sources are increasingly incentivizing innovations that are intended to lower costs and improve the quality of learning.

For example, through grants from the Trade Adjustment Assistance Community College and Career Training Program (TAACCCT), funding is available to integrate career-focused education that accelerates and contextualizes remediation, advances technology-enabled learning, and implements competency-based learning assessment.[11] While colleges must show fidelity to these oftentimes competing agendas, there is an opportunity to "redesign, reinvent, reset who they are, what they do, and how students learn."[12]

Quality, Learning, and Attainment

One might argue that quality as described in this book could simply be considered as just another element of the attainment agenda. If expectations for students are clear via well-articulated learning outcomes, students will succeed since their work will have purpose and meaning relative to the degree. Clear expectations are the *essential ingredient* for most students who enroll at community colleges.

For example, a first-generation student with very little prior knowledge of higher education will benefit from a thoughtful and coherent educational pathway. With the end always in sight, beginning an academic program, and persisting in that program, becomes easier. Likewise, students who initially select one program and then look to change their major will benefit from well-articulated academic and technical paths.

Students who are pursuing technical degrees leading directly to jobs in specific industries appreciate efforts to bridge academia with the workforce through a clear framework of student proficiencies defining what a student will know and be able to do at the conclusion of their studies.

What follows in the succeeding chapters is an exploration of advances in teaching, learning, and assessment, and suggestions for engaging faculty in reimaging them collectively for the purpose of helping many more students to achieve their education and career goals.

Chapter 2, through the lens of new challenges for accreditation, explores the relationship between learning, persistence, and completion, moving beyond institutional compliance to student learning as the focal point for quality, considering equity and excellence in the context of quality, and the potential for expanding modes and providers to address equity and excellence. There are already leaders in these areas with the courage to envision change and the will to begin to advance change.

It also suggests a new role for accreditation in higher education. Instead of the traditional approach of accreditation as certification of quality, accreditors can become the catalysts for the evolution to student-centeredness that our colleges so desperately need. Instead of simply enabling financial aid transactions, accreditors must assume a transformative leadership role if their relevance is to be preserved and enhanced. We argue for this transformation.

Chapter 3 explores the evolution of higher education to competency-based education models from the current course and credit model. The chapter begins with a comparison of various definitions of competency-based models and then moves to examining three community colleges that are currently applying elements of competency-based education.

Chapter 4 lays out a comprehensive plan for building a campus culture of student learning assessment. The chapter describes a comprehensive, community college–wide assessment system, beginning with a flowchart tool to engage stakeholders in dialogue around assessment of student learning. The chapter concludes by offering practical applications and strategies in the development and enhancement of a campus assessment system and culture.

Chapter 5 closes the book with a discussion of the importance of faculty in leading transitions to improved teaching and learning. Traditional notions of the role of faculty in improving student learning are challenged and strategies for making faculty the centerpiece of redesigned teaching and learning strategies are explored. Then the reader is offered a draft plan for engaging faculty in productive conversations in order to avoid becoming mired in traditional academic debates that inevitably lead to frustration and impede progress in improving student learning.

In each of these chapters, the premise is the same. All of higher education, with community colleges leading the way, must sense and respond to the need to evolve to serve a new and increasingly diverse student body that requires all kinds of new approaches to higher education to realize their potential. In order to ensure equity in the form of economic opportunity for current and future generations, facility with U.S. culture and systems for immigrants, and provide demonstrable learning outcomes that position students for success, it is time for new models to take hold. That is the urgency of now.

NOTES

1. Robert B. Barr and John Tagg, "From Teaching to Learning—A New Paradigm for Undergraduate Education," *Change* 27 (1995).

2. Stan Ikenberry and George Kuh, "Using Evidence to Make a Difference," *National Institute for Learning Outcomes Assessment*, accessed March 9, 2015, https://illinois.edu/blog/view/915/128556.

3. George B. Vaughn, *The Community College Story* (New York: Rowman and Littlefield, 2006).

4. "2015 Community College Fact Sheet," American Association of Community Colleges, accessed March 9, 2015, http://www.aacc.nche.edu/AboutCC/Documents/FactSheet2015.pdf.

5. "Renewing the American Dream: The College Completion Agenda," whitehouse.gov, accessed March 9, 2015, http://www.whitehouse.gov/blog/2011/10/05/renewing-american-dream-college-completion-agenda, Christine J, McPhail, *The Completion Agenda: A Call to Action* (Washington, D.C.: American Association of Community Colleges), Gary Rhoades, "The Incomplete Completion Agenda: Implications for Academe and the Academy," *Liberal Education* 98 (2012).

6. "Degree Qualifications Profile," Lumina Foundation, accessed October 22, 2014, http://degreeprofile.org/read-the-dqp/, "Mozilla Open Badges," Mozilla, accessed March 9, 2015, http://openbadges.org/earn/, Paul Fain, "Taking the Direct Path," *Inside Higher Education*, February 21, 2014, accessed March 9, 2015, https://www.insidehighered.com/news/2014/02/21/

direct-assessment-and-feds-take-competency-based-education, "Adult Learners Guide to PLA," American Council on Education, accessed March 9, 2015, http://www.acenet.edu/news-room/Pages/Adult-Learners-Guide-to-PLA.aspx, and "VALUE Rubric Development Project," Association of American Colleges and Universities, accessed March 9, 2015, http://www.aacu.org/value/rubrics.

7. "Federal Student Aid: Experimental Sites Initiative," U.S. Department of Education, accessed November 1, 2014, https://experimentalsites.ed.gov/exp/approved.html.

8. Amy Latinen, *Cracking the Credit Hour* (Washington, D.C.: New America Foundation, 2012).

9. "Institutional Retention and Graduation Rates for Undergraduate Students," National Center for Education Statistics, accessed March 9, 2015, http://nces.ed.gov/programs/coe/indicator_cva.asp.

10. "Building American Skills Through Community Colleges," whitehouse.gov, accessed March 9, 2015, http://www.whitehouse.gov/issues/education/higher-education/building-american-skills-through-community-colleges.

11. "TAACCCT Program Summary," United States Department of Labor, accessed March 9, 2015, http://www.doleta.gov/taaccct/.

12. "AACC 21st Century Center," American Association of Community Colleges, accessed March 9, 2015, http://www.aacc.nche.edu/AboutCC/21st_century/Documents/AACC_21stCenturyBro_low.pdf.

2

THE ACCOUNTABLE INSTITUTION

From Compliance to Learning

Lynn E. Priddy

In 2004, Lumina Foundation and seven founding partners launched Achieving the Dream with twenty-seven "Round 1" community colleges focused on cultivating institutional transformation with a decisive goal of increasing student success, particularly that of low-income students and students of color. Focused on closing learning and achievement gaps through new strategies and interventions, "the partners involved believed that the cultural and institutional changes themselves would engender changes in student outcomes" and bring equity and excellence to fruition.[1]

Today, degree attainment, or the "completion agenda," dominates definitions of accountability, spurred by President Obama's challenge to achieve eight million additional degrees by 2020,[2] a Gates Foundation 2020 goal to double the degrees held by low-income students while lowering costs and sustaining access and quality,[3] and Lumina Foundation's call to increase the number of Americans with postsecondary credentials to 60 percent by 2025.[4]

These goals, however, face formidable racial, cultural, and socioeconomic divides that play out in disconcerting patterns of educational stratification. The divide begins with the type of institutions attended.

In 2006, blacks and Hispanics together totaled only 12 percent of students at the most selective institutions. In comparison, whites constituted 75 percent.[5] In fact, Carnevale and Strohl note that "82 percent of new white enrollments have gone to the 468 most selective colleges, while 72 percent of new Hispanic enrollment and 68 percent of new African-American enrollment have gone to the two-year and four-year open-access schools."[6]

Second, stratification has worsened over the past thirty years. "In 1982, students from the top socioeconomic quarter of the population made up 24 percent of the students at community colleges; by 2006, that had dropped to 16 percent."[7]

Third, resource allocation follows the upper income quartiles. From 1999 to 2009, "per-pupil total operating expenditures increased by almost $14,000 for private research universities, while public community colleges saw just a $1 increase (in 2009 dollars)."[8] Not surprisingly, these patterns impact degree attainment.

In 2010, only 11 percent of bottom income quartile and 49 percent of second and third quartile students would earn a four-year degree by age twenty-four compared to 79 percent of students from higher-income families.[9] In fact, since 1977 baccalaureate degree completion rates have increased by more than 62 percent for those students with families in the top two quartiles of income, while increasing less than 10 percent for those in the bottom half.[10] Dropout rates continue to hover near 70 percent and completion rates struggle to reach 49 percent at two- and four-year open-access institutions compared to 82 percent completion at the most selective four-year colleges.[11]

In fact, the Pell Institute for the Study of Opportunity in Higher Education cites income-based inequality in educational attainment as a central obstacle to achieving the 2020 goal, and indicates that decreasing income-based attainment gaps must become a central focus of federal education policy.[12] The Organization for Economic Cooperation and Development Secretary-General Angel Gurría cites income-based inequality, the highest educational costs worldwide, and slowing social mobility and educational attainment as the greatest threats to U.S. long-term prosperity.[13]

When introduced, detractors criticized the completion agenda as credential attainment absent quality and void of learning. That accusation might have been fair early in these initiatives, but not in 2014.

For example, Goal 2025 urgently presses for a full social movement around students, their learning, college degrees, and national workforce needs. As Samuel Cargile from Lumina Foundation states in the introduction, the urgency of now moves the definition of accountability beyond access and completion to equity and excellence and compels community colleges toward reforms targeting deeper student learning, greater degree attainment, and flexible education pathways. In the spirit of urgency, this chapter proposes four tenets:

1. Quality of learning, quality of persistence, and quality of completion are interdependent. All matter, but learning matters most.
2. Current accountability measures are tightening down on institutions, focusing on compliance just at a time when equity and excellence demand the opposite—a focus on innovation in learning.
3. Achieving equity and excellence requires new definitions and measures for quality and accountability related to student learning.
4. Achieving equity and excellence in student learning requires redesigning the educational experience without boundaries as to who, when, what, or how.

To allow for ideas not yet fully tested or captured, quotes from personal communications with several individuals who think idealistically, act boldly, and embrace reality pepper this chapter. All are educators who push the edge and don't back away.

ON THE EDGE OF ACCOUNTABILITY AND LEARNING

For most community colleges, quality, accountability, and the centrality of student learning have been intertwined commitments since their institutional beginnings in the 1960s and 1970s, unfolding through the institutional effectiveness and student learning assessment movements. In *Accountability and the Community College: Directions for the 70s,* a paper commissioned by the American Association of Junior Colleges (AAJC), Roueche, Baker, and Brownell argued that the time had come for community colleges to meet the challenges of accountability and to achieve ways to demonstrate institutional effectiveness.[14]

In the next decade, Thompson, Alfred, and Lowther proposed a quality systems model for community college productivity.[15] Hudgins expanded their ideas to incorporate continuous quality improvement principles, stressing institutional renewal and cultural change through effectiveness processes demonstrated by measurable results for stakeholders.[16]

By the midnineties, the American Association of Community Colleges (AACC) had developed thirteen core indicators of community college effectiveness.[17]

Similarly, in 1997, Roueche, Johnson, and Roueche expanded these indicators into a survey of community college approaches to institutional effectiveness. In their seminal book, *Embracing the Tiger,* the authors provide a broad-based review of these survey results accompanied by overarching recommendations and seven detailed case studies of strategies and models.[18]

Student learning, persistence, completion, and placement are not new accountability measures for community colleges. Even the early effectiveness models espoused them as performance indicators with the true test being achieved, demonstrated student learning.[19] In fact, the allegedly new idea of competency-based education as a replacement for time-constant measures thrived nearly forty years ago in the 1976 monograph *Time as the Variable, Achievement as the Constant: Competency-Based Instruction in the Community College.*[20] Community colleges have been leaders in embracing quality improvement processes and have capitalized on accreditation processes and foundation- or organization-sponsored programs to catalyze effectiveness efforts and to demonstrate accountability for students and their learning.

When the Higher Learning Commission of the North Central Association launched the Academic Quality Improvement Program (AQIP), an alternative accreditation process based on continuous quality improvement principles, community colleges were among the first to join and continue to comprise the largest majority of participating institutions.[21]

A general review of improvement initiatives published by regional accreditors and the Center for Community College Student Engagement
shows a strong pattern of reform. Over the past five years, community
colleges have focused on revamping remedial education, establishing
new entry pathways and first-year curricular sequences, integrating
general education and degree field learning outcomes, and using degree
frameworks such as the Tuning USA project and the Degree Qualifications Profile (DQP) to map learning across and between traditional
structures (courses, co-curricular, programs, workplaces).[22]

In addition, community colleges have pursued intrusive advising and
coaching, high-impact pedagogical practices, predictive analytics, complex assessment, and new modalities for faculty, student, and employer
engagement and collaborations that upend traditional roles.[23] If commitment, effort, and organizational learning are valid measures, community colleges exemplify accountability.

However, despite the considerable investment and initiative, these
reforms have yet to meet accountability or student success goals. Ten
years after its launch, the Achieving the Dream, Inc. (ATD) national
reform network now encompasses more than two hundred institutions serving nearly four million students across thirty-four states and
the District of Columbia, with hundreds of strategies aimed at broad
institutional changes leading to clear gains in student learning and
completion.[24]

The results detailed in the April 2014 report on ATD's progress re-
veal the complexity of the completion challenge. Although the findings
document sound organizational effectiveness systems, data capacity,
and pertinent cultural changes, an analysis of six outcomes, including
degree attainment, indicated little to no broad change, with the excep-
tion of gains in developmental English.[25]

Reponses to the findings by the researchers and others point to the
need to focus on the teaching and learning outcomes of specific student
subgroups, to more broadly and deeply engage the faculty, as will be
discussed in chapter 5, and to scale projects to the full system to achieve
the broader learning and completion impact intended.[26] "Many colleges
are doing valuable work, but rarely at the scale needed for substantive
improvements."[27] A sound foundation for reform exists, but the real
reform remains ahead.

Sandy Shugart, president of Valencia Community College, proposes that the real reform is learning and that the completion agenda must first be a learning agenda with the secondary benefit being degree attainment.

> [G]iven that the national goal of increasing the percentage of working Americans with a degree depends very heavily on enrolling and graduating many more nontraditional students, we might draw special attention to the challenges of the community colleges, where more than half of all college students begin their educations, and where 80 percent of the underrepresented, the poor, and the first-generation students are served. If they are to be enfranchised at all . . . we need them to experience pathways to deep learning, progression, graduation, and further education. . . . The degree is a means to an end. Relevant, deep learning is the end.[28]

Roberta Teahen, associate provost, Ferris State University, extends Shugart's argument:

> The current political and accountability agenda speaks to quality, accountability, and completion as a means for achieving national goals for educational and economic prosperity. However, learning is the more powerful driver and the more difficult challenge. What will it take to ensure low-income, black, Hispanic, and working adult students really learn, *really learn*? We've passed them on through high school without the learning necessary; by doing so, the education system has shortchanged their futures. If honest, we realize our developmental programs still remain more barrier than bridge; attrition in these programs is nearly unforgiveable. Add to these that Title IV too often becomes the new welfare and educational debt the new mortgage. This isn't about breaking the glass ceiling; it's about lifting the floorboards and getting citizens above the line. It's learning to the proficiency that breaks through, not simply accumulates courses and credits for a credential. If learning, *real learning that leads to social change and a sense of belonging in a field* occurs, completion will follow, and frankly, completion is a bonus.[29]

Quality of learning, quality of persistence, and quality of completion all matter; but learning matters most. The three together become a new "iron triangle" of accountability defined as student success. Learning is primary, for without it, the focus is productivity versus excellence. Administrators and faculty, however, may advise that completion—albeit a significant gap—is the lesser challenge as few colleges can yet speak clearly to learning gains.

To illustrate, institutions have worked to assess and improve student learning for twenty-five years. When asked by accreditors what they've accomplished, institutions answer with dozens of curricular changes, outcomes revisions, and new measures and methodologies. However, when asked, for example, to what degree mastery of a learning outcome such as ethical reasoning or analytical writing has improved for Pell-eligible African American males as a result, the answers are few. Significant changes—improvements to the educational enterprise—have been made, but the goal of equity and excellence remains elusive. The goal may be elusive, but equity and excellence remains ever more critical to the nation, according to Margaretta Brédé Mathis.

> For the United States to be competitive globally, increasing the number of students who complete a certificate or degree that is aligned with higher-value-added labor market skill demands will be critical. Unfortunately, many educational institutions are not equipped to offer the necessary student and academic support, policies, practices, content and care that are required to help students succeed. Furthermore, tailoring educational offerings to meet the needs of diverse learners will require new ways of working with students, faculty, administrators, trustees and other stakeholders to increase student success. To be competitive, the nation and its institutions will need to be responsive to changing labor-market demands. To be domestically and globally productive and responsible, educational institutions will need to build awareness and understanding about global citizenship, respectfully open conversations and minds to embrace changing student populations and learn to adapt to diverse learning needs.[30]

Equity and excellence in learning, persistence, and completion require much deeper systemic changes both within and beyond institutions, including release from time-based boundaries—credit hours, courses, terms, funding, even degrees. Collective learning across recent initiatives points to the need for:

- Institutional transformation around students and their learning.
- Redesign of education around the new ways people learn, engage, and achieve career and life goals.

- Comprehensive approaches, collaborations, and shared responsibilities that cut across institutions, states, accreditors, business and industry, nonprofit organizations, and the federal government.[31]

As effective as community colleges are as reformers, these systemic shifts require much broader collaboration and a willingness to cross traditional institutional and credential boundaries. In addition, these shifts won't be achieved without support from state and federal policy, a rollback of regulation, and systems revolution and realignment.[32]

Unfortunately, policy and regulation seem, philosophically, to be in regression. Achieving equity and excellence depends on finding ways to intervene and address two significant challenges: increased regulation and focus on compliance requirements versus quality measures, and the rift and role confusion between accreditation and the federal government.

QUALITY, ACCOUNTABILITY, AND THE REALITY OF REGULATION AND COMPLIANCE

While the need for more quality credentials is great, resources are few, and the public grows increasingly dubious about the costs, quality, and claims of higher education. Shugart offers sobering words about current perceptions:

> We are being asked to achieve much better results with fewer resources, to engage a needier student population in an atmosphere of serious skepticism where all journalism is yellow and our larger society no longer exempts our institutions (nor us) from the deep distrust that has grown toward all institutions.[33]

The U.S. three-pronged approach to assuring and advancing higher education quality (federal government authorizes higher education, states approve institutions, and accreditors validate quality) has been the envy of other countries, the majority of which have a single appointed ministry with authority for all three roles.[34]

According to Paul Gaston, accreditors should advocate for innovation, document institutional experiments, and focus on finding processes for strong institutions to engage in non-traditional collaborations, degree constructs, role reversals, and other strategies testing current mental models of higher education and what might be achieved in terms of student learning and student success.[35]

Based on his points, the past decade would have been an ideal time for state and federal agencies to figure out how to suspend time, and for Title IV regulations to allow for open innovation focused on new designs that actually do confront the learning and completion shortfalls of significant numbers of American citizens. Instead, in October 2010, the Department of Education published its definition of the credit hour and the new expectations for accreditors to monitor how institutions delivered their courses and programs in compliance with this definition.[36]

Rising college prices, decreased public funding, a culture that operates on debt, and questions of institutional integrity and transparency have made cost and compliance paramount, with a hostile climate for experimentation. Compliance now defines the accountable institution; productivity, efficiency, and affordability have become proxies for quality. A single representative example sets the context.

A community college determines to launch a new aviation program based on feasibility studies and discussions with employers, faculty and staff, boards, and community leaders. The institution has already been in discussions for months with a Federal Aviation Administration–approved (FAA) flight school based in another state and a different FAA-approved ground school just across state lines, ten miles away, that partners with the flight school and shares instructors. The plan proposes a competency-based hybrid program offered 60 percent online and 50 percent face-to-face on location in the two other states. The program allows flexibility for students to take as much as 75 percent either face-to-face or online; military pilots have special accelerated and prior learning assessment options. Depending on the institution, state, and regional or national accreditors, state approval may be necessary and required prior to screening and contractual arrangement approval by the accreditor(s), as well as competency-based direct assessment or "significant departure" program modification approval from the accreditor. This may be followed by requirements for external certifying agency confirmation, notification to or E-app approval by the Department of Education, state authorization from all states from which the institution expects students to originate, and perhaps even the accreditor's approval for a new campus or degree center.

Through it all, each approval entity wants very similar, but not the same, data and information, and they often want it via different formulas, slightly different formats, covering different time periods, and inclusive of different cohorts and numbers of students. Accreditors approve the program; appropriate notifications are sent to the government. It is twenty months and several hundred thousand dollars later, as much as three years from the first conversation, that the program is fully launched. Munch's *The Scream* serves as a fitting metaphor.[37]

ACCESS, AFFORDABILITY, QUALITY, AND ACCOUNTABILITY

Today, it's trite even to say that "the demand for accountability in higher education" is a nebulous phrase: Accountable for what? To whom? Based on what? Whereas hints of the regulatory future appeared in the early 1990s, the future arrived fully in September 2006 with a report from the Commission on the Future of Higher Education, more commonly known as the Spellings Commission and the Spellings report, named for the then Secretary of Education.

Instead of targeting institutions directly, the report and follow-up issue papers launched a frontal attack on accreditation, its credibility, and its capacity to assure the quality of higher education through self-regulation. The report also cited lack of transparency and deficiency of meaningful information on academic effectiveness, institutional integrity, and student learning and success.[38] Within months of the secretary's report, the field saw a renewed proliferation of articles on institutional performance that revealed an emerging regulatory fervor and carried a common theme on higher education's lack of cultural competence for accountability or educational quality.[39]

Until recently, few argued with definitions of institutional quality that gave primacy to faculty and administrators. In other words, quality has been assumed within higher education despite the fact that the enterprise is self-regulated through accreditation via peer review and carried out in the context of the institution's mission, purposes, and students.

Quality assurance and quality improvement have comprised the foundation for evaluation; peer reviewers have brought experience that informed effective critiques for both purposes with the focus resting on improvement.[40] For more than a hundred years, regional accreditation has played a vital role in furthering the advancement of higher education; peer review of institutional and education excellence has led to many of the gains cited above. Core tenets of accreditation have included self-regulation; institutional autonomy; mission-driven evaluation; diversity of purposes, students, educational programs, and services; and peer review.

Quality has rested on educational excellence aligned with distinctive goals and purposes, effective teaching and learning, integrity of mission and governance, appropriate resources and services, planning and evaluation leading to ongoing improvement, and capacity to sustain and improve institutional and educational quality.

Although accreditors cite a track record of success on these issues, these central foci of institutional evaluation have become fodder for external criticism that portrays peer review as "good-old-boy dodgeball," condemn assessment criteria as holistic to the point of being useless for defining what is "good enough," and decry mission and autonomy as excuses for lack of clear, bright line standards. The infrequency of accreditation reviews, the inability to identify the bad actors, and a paucity of real information on evaluation findings round out the issues cited.[41]

A recent rash of regulations, on the other hand, has led to new questions: what is quality and who gets to define it? In a 2009 gathering of accreditors and members of the American Council on Higher Education, a prominent U.S. senator began a presentation on the increase in federal and state regulation of higher education while standing beside a single banker's box. He addressed increased state and federal regulation and reporting, drawing comparisons between health care and education. As he did, stagehands stacked banker's box on top of banker's box until at the end, the senator was dwarfed in size, making his point verbally and visually.

In 2010, the Office of Postsecondary Education (OPE) directed the largest regional accreditor to establish minimum expectations for quality within the accrediting criteria—and to require them of all institutions.[42]

In that same year, along with its definition of the credit hour, the Department of Education enacted an additional fifteen new regulations.[43]

In response to attacks on accreditation, the American Council on Higher Education convened a National Task Force on Institutional Accreditation. The resulting 2012 report defends the central premises and promises of the distinctly American quality assurance and improvement process, but at a cost. The Task Force's first principle for accreditors makes clear the priority.

> *Emphasize assuring quality.* The first and most important theme of the Task Force recommendations is the need to make certain that accreditation standards and review processes are squarely focused on assuring educational quality. . . . When the current practices of mission-centered, peer-based review first emerged, the primary purpose of accreditation was to promote institutional improvement. This emphasis properly continues today. But pressing demands for more and better evidence of institutional quality from a range of stakeholders—government, business, and the public at large—compels higher education to place an equivalent emphasis on examining and assuring institutional quality.[44]

Of significance is how the report defends key premises of accreditation, but turns the focus of accreditors to quality assurance. Although it may have been a move of necessity, the shift diminished accreditation's long-standing stronghold as a leader in higher education improvement, reform, and innovation, and set up additional barriers to institutional redesign as accreditors responded, inevitably, with stronger assurance systems. In May of 2014, the federal government launched an investigation of more than fifty institutions and their Title IX practices.[45] In late 2014, the federal government effectively closed multiple institutions without the benefit of accreditor influence or legislative review.[46]

This short set of examples illustrates a nasty and potentially damaging cycle: increased distrust in higher education has led to increased distrust in accreditation, has led to increased regulation, has led to increased scrutiny by accreditors and others, has led to more press on punitive actions by accreditors, has led to negative press on institutions, cycling back to an increased distrust of higher education. External agencies are "tightening down" on institutions with more rules, boundaries, and definitions of credits and degrees just at a time when Goal 2025 demands institutions to experiment, innovate, and test strategies that cross boundaries, undo definitions, and break rules.

Ironically, the external agencies use the completion agenda as a driving force for the shifting character of accreditation as "the Department of Education slowly emerges as the accreditor-in-chief, with regional accreditors becoming its enforcement arms. Their focus, first in the for-profit sector but now in all sectors, has been retention and graduation rates—the college completion agenda." [47]

Growing distrust continues to beget increased regulation despite all the innovations and their possibilities for student success. President Swarthout of Northland Pioneer College describes the impact:

> I'm tired of going to battle every single day to preserve the future of students the college serves. Funding and compliance requirements must achieve a realistic balance. I dream that a united dashboard for compliance is in place with a limited, unified, automatically calculated number of data points to rein in the literally thousands of person-hours we spend on this annually. Example: Our crime report is now 164 pages. Just this week it took 15 hours of three pricey administrators, not counting attorney and staff support time. We are small, extremely rural, no sports, no residence halls, no fraternities or sororities. Of the 164 pages, only 3 pages contained anything but zeroes. The emphasis must be on student education and learning. I don't choose to draw swords with every legislator and compliance officer who crosses my path but I must and will. I'm equally tired of seeing statistics that say my students are not a success. Learn what we do before you count them as failures, please! [48]

In fact, community colleges have been accountable to the definitions of quality long held by academe and most accreditors, exemplified in myriad initiatives summarized above that tell a story of deep responsibility for students, their learning, and their educational and professional success. However, accountability through aspirations, effort, and a focus on improvement offers ill-fitting results for measuring up (or down) to bright line minimum standards and definitions of quality focused on assurance and compliance. In fact, compliance and regulation drive institutions away from being able to deal with equity and excellence for marginalized populations. These students become an institutional risk.

By one standard, the accountable institution is one that graduates the most and achieves 100 percent compliance with states, accreditors, and the Department of Education. By another standard, the accountable institution is the college at which students learn the most, the institution that steadily improves the percentage of students who achieve increasingly deeper levels of learning that they demonstrate and apply in future degrees, in the community, and/or in the workplace.

> Despite the best intentions of legislators, government policies often force the focus of institutions away from the mission of student learning. . . . Decisions cannot be based on past practices when the world is changing so rapidly. The mission of higher education is student learning, and all of our policies, procedures and practices must be aligned with that mission if our institutions are to remain relevant.[49]

Linda Darling-Hammond's critique of the Department of Education's No Child Left Behind initiative includes a statement that could become distressingly true in higher education.

> . . . the Act's regulations have caused a number . . . to abandon their thoughtful diagnostic assessment and accountability systems—replacing instructionally rich, improvement-oriented systems with more rote-oriented, punishment-driven approaches—and it has thrown many high performing and steadily improving schools into chaos rather than helping them remain focused and deliberate in their ongoing efforts to serve students well.[50]

Only significant policy and regulatory changes—or forums for innovation protected from them—offer a way to honor regulation and compliance, yet keep a steady focus on students and their learning.

FROM COMPLIANCE TO LEARNING

Community colleges currently lead and must lead in moving higher education toward Goal 2025 and are doing so through initiatives such as Achieving the Dream, Completion by Design, Tuning USA, the Degree Qualifications Profile, Competency-Based Education Network, Mathways, and the AAC&U Roadmap Project.[51] While policy makers and institutional leaders focus on highlighting, sharing, and scaling best practices at successful community colleges, the true need is to ". . . go beyond that limited approach and offer bold and innovative thinking that is also efficacious."[52]

Demography is not destiny; however, radical redesign of institutions and funding innovations for better serving and graduating underrepresented populations need to be celebrated to avoid prioritizing selectivity over access, excellence, and equity.[53] "Given the rapidly changing demographics of higher education, such realignment is imperative."[54]

According to Wheatley, systems contain their own solutions. "Somewhere in the system are people already practicing solutions that others think are impossible."[55] She cautions that change occurs more often through revelation than revolution, emerging more in the creation than in the implementation of new designs. Jonathan Keiser, associate vice chancellor of city colleges of Chicago, echoes Wheatley's admonition and states succinctly:

> We launch initiatives. Some create short-term change, others longer term, many suffocate under their own weight. I'm beginning to think it's in doing the initiative versus implementing results that is the way forward. During the initiative, we are open, thinking about the future, re-imagining, and re-forming our relationships and ways of thinking and working together that reflect the culture we want to become. Then we implement the initiative, and it ends up being sucked back into the old processes, structures, and mindsets. We use new tools to old ends. Then it's precarious, for without the shift in culture, the forward-looking design and new ways of working have the potential to become nothing but busy-work and more documentation. The same is true of accountability efforts—Any effort to hold higher education accountable TO quality versus responsible FOR learning is likely to become busy work for someone else's agenda if we don't understand and value the criteria on which we are being judged.[56]

In *Reframing Retention Strategy for Institutional Improvement*, David Kalsbeek provides an analogy. He argues that current approaches to improve persistence and completion are perhaps not moving the needle because they are limited to single versus comprehensive efforts, stuck in and reactions to the real need: changing the system, structures, and policies completely versus innovating within them.

He advocates creating "structures of opportunity" through a 4Ps (profile, progress, process, promise) framework that challenges sacred cows, long-standing assumptions, and core institutional structures and systems, including administrative policies, faculty and administrator roles, marketing and branding assumptions, academic calendars, program prioritization and pricing, teaching and learning patterns, and curricular pathways across institutions.[57]

Reinforcing Kalsbeek's systemic approach, Terry O'Banion proposes coherent, intentionally designed student pathways through the entirety of the educational experience. These pathways then determine institutional priorities, frame strategic plans, and realign college work so that "what colleges do is what students do and what students do is what colleges do."[58]

Both Kalsbeek and O'Banion support full redesign of the institution, its policies and processes, and its culture and practices around students and their learning. These perspectives are echoed in Daniel Kim's envisioned systemic change that he contends is necessary to overcome an organization's "patterned blindness" of the ways it has always operated.

In *Organizing for Learning,* Kim postulates that most organizations do not recognize how comprehensively different they must become and that they fail to scale reforms tested on parts of the institution to the whole. Thus, despite the efforts to change, the institution leaves intact both the overall pattern of how the organization functions and how the culture collectively sees its work.

Going on, Kim asserts that institutions must create and define in detail a completely new theory of work and culture in order to break old patterns and shift existing ways of thinking. Theory-building allows institutions to see conceptually what hasn't yet been practiced or experienced, just espoused. Detailed theories create pathways from individual initiatives that improve parts of the organization to comprehensive changes that fully redefine how it functions.[59]

In another 2025 initiative, Stanford University's Hasso Plattner Institute of Design has opened a public conversation to reimagine undergraduate learning in pursuit of a completely new theory of the educational enterprise. Although Stanford students may be vastly different from most, the four provocations resonate with community college lifelong learning efforts:

Open loop. This imagines the college experience as a series of "loops" over a lifetime. This plan would admit students at eighteen but give them six years of access to residential learning opportunities, to use any time in their life. It would allow alumni to return midcareer for professional development and new students to get real-life work experience.

Paced education. This abolishes the class year and replaces it with adaptive, personalized learning that allows students to move through phases of learning at their own pace. The goal is to help students make better choices about what they want to study and understand their own learning style.

Axis flip. Rather than traditional academic disciplines, the curriculum would be organized around common and transferable skills that could be used over the course of a lifetime. Schools and departments would be reorganized around "competency hubs" so that there would be deans of scientific analysis, quantitative reasoning, moral and ethical reasoning, communication effectiveness, among others.

Purpose learning. Instead of majors, students would declare a "mission" to help them find meaning and purpose behind their studies.[60]

The urgency of now is the urgency of innovation and excellence in learning. If community colleges are to lead the way in fulfilling learning and credential shortfalls for working adults often underserved in the current systems, the following considerations and propositions offer places to begin.

Considerations and Provocative Propositions

Two types of propositions follow, those focused on regulatory and compliance quandaries, and those focused on teaching, learning, and the complete redesign of institutions. Both sets challenge community college leaders to rethink boundaries. Both also require leaders adept at "inventing the future while dealing with the past."[61]

Reclaim Regional Accreditation's Historical Focus

Accreditation criteria still place educational excellence and student academic achievement central to institutional quality even while having to absorb new compliance-based regulation. Accrediting agencies remain key to honoring compliance while focusing on learning; they still frame what defines quality, who gets to be part of that definition, and what constitutes a credential. Although seen as a weakness by some, accreditation's membership structure provides a forum for collaboration and shared learning that could rebalance the compliance-assurance-improvement continuum and even lead to new means for credentials and credentialing.

Accreditors maintain a perspective across thousands of institutions offering tremendous potential for mining information from patterns of unsound practice to flourishing innovations common to diverse types of institutions. Accreditors have access to the revelations and creations of new designs referred to by Wheatley and have the influence, noted by Keiser, to hold higher education responsible for learning versus simply accountable to quality. With thousands of institutions, nonetheless, accrediting agencies can lose touch with all but the members currently in crisis (too few "watch lists" focus on good and great institutions), a pattern reinforced by recent state and federal actions and a pattern that means accrediting processes have fattened around assurance and compliance.

Despite the current compliance mantra, most regional accreditors already have what might be called "split and focus" processes: i.e., reviews that split out evaluation of quality assurance and federal compliance from critique and recognition of quality improvement, emerging practice, and innovation. Three considerations describe more intrusive collaboration among regional accreditors and their member institutions.

1. Fulfill compliance and assurance requirements through routinely reported, streamlined data and information indicators shared with states and the federal government, and allow appropriate variation for institutional mission, purpose, and students. Technology-based compliance and assurance processes occurring routinely, frequently, and in the background, unless otherwise warranted, reduce redundancy and burden. More importantly, they reduce the focus on compliance and assurance by managing these factors automatically unless an institution needs direct intervention on baseline measures.

2. With compliance managed through routine technology-driven indicator monitoring, accreditors could rebalance the dual processes. Instead of splitting out assurance and improvement so as to increase the attention to assurance and compliance, the reverse could be true: i.e., splitting out so as to increase the focus on improved student learning, on mining and analysis of data and information to inform policy and decision-making, and on findings across thousands of institutions that lead to improvement and innovation.

3. Create forums for novel collaborations among institutions and including even broader constituencies to expand funded projects of philanthropic organizations and state initiatives, as well as demonstration projects and experimental sites of the Department of Education.

Thus, instead of setting up barriers to innovation, accrediting agencies facilitate knowledge generation and dissemination across quality assurance and improvement processes and convene the collaborative endeavors to test, experiment with, and disseminate the new definitions and practices of high-impact, high-integrity, high-quality education.

Continue Pressing for Alternative Funding Approaches

A plethora of articles, arguments, models, and methodologies address changing, expanding, or blowing up current higher education funding models. Disagreements continue on declines, increases, or cost-shifting of state funds, but the continued reliance on tuition for most institutions is undeniable. The Century Task Force on Preventing Community Colleges from Becoming Separate and Unequal recommends K-12, Title I–type financing.[62] Others vehemently disagree. Meanwhile, states push forward seeking local solutions.

The National Center for Higher Education Management System report for Complete College America contains principles for designing outcomes-based funding that cut across the debates, as long as parties agree that resource allocation should be based on accountability for value-added learning and other outcomes.[63]

The urgency of resolving funding is particularly tangible for racially and economically disadvantaged individuals who gamble that the debt acquired to achieve a degree translates to a future salary adequate to pay it back. Although the upper quartiles may now enjoy economic recovery, U.S. economic prosperity demands educational prosperity. Both depend on significant shifts in educational financing, educational attainment, and social mobility.

Create New Learning and Credential Pathways

The case studies and examples in later chapters of this book attest to the effectiveness of redesigned learning pathways. Unconstrained by courses, credits, and even degrees, faculty and others create a progression of scaffolded learning customized to student needs and goals through carefully designed sequences and combinations of competencies, proficiencies, and mastery experiences. Learning progressions discard credit-bound ideas (30 credits to a certificate, 60 credits to an associate degree) and allow students to step in, step out, circle back, and continue on toward personalized goals. In fact, learning progressions allow students to define completion based on their goals and their timing versus a degree status sheet or a maximum time frame.

When done well, learning pathways integrate disciplines, general education, and the major. They also cut across institutional and workplace boundaries. Learning progressions are several generations evolved from articulations and transfer agreements. Although the penchant of institutions may be to try the adoption of pieces of these improvements, comprehensive approaches may serve better based on emerging findings.[64]

Community colleges will have to invent the future while co-opting practices from the present and past. The distributed curricula, block transfer agreements, prior learning assessment, and even remedial education dissolve into a natural rate-variable progression of learning versus specific boxes of defined kinds, levels, and paces of learning, as well as judgments of their worth or expected order of attainment. Developmental education is a case in point, as explained by Robert Mundhenk, former chief academic officer and current senior scholar at the Higher Learning Commission.

Colleges are now honestly looking at developmental and remedial education, as well as what actual skills different degrees require. Too many remedial courses have been designed for transfer. Everyone needs mathematics, perhaps some statistics, and some basic algebra, but College Algebra? Does a welding student need to be able to write a ten-page paper?

Even if we think so, we've been really bad at explaining why she does—or why she needs two semesters of remedial before she can take a course that will enable her to write that paper.[65]

Soon other more difficult conversations will be needed about depth and breadth of inquiry, disciplines and majors, general education, and faculty roles. Coherent learning progressions allow for customized credential pathways but are complex, ever-changing, non-linear, and require masterful teaching, coaching, and assessing. Faculty hold an even more important role in all of these new designs.

Replace Roles with Relationships and Partitions with Transitions

"Something there is that doesn't love a wall, [t]hat wants it down," writes poet Robert Frost.[66] Higher education thrives on boundaries of all kinds that limit learning pathways. Walls, silos, and boundaries in higher education are time-based (credits, courses, semesters, degrees), resource-based (Title IV regulations, scholarships, required positions), level-based (badge, certificate, certification, associate, baccalaureate, and so on), entity-based (high school, community college, four-year institution, comprehensive university, etc.), role-based (administrator, faculty, adjunct instructor, etc.), and there are many others.

Michael Chipps, president of Northeast Community College in Nebraska, thrives on taking down walls:

You'll hear me talk a lot about transitions versus partitions and about relationships and learning without these institutional boundaries we're so fond of. We're in every high school; they are all in on our campus. We're together in career academies. We're together with multiple nearby private four-year institutions and public universities. We share degrees and diplomas. Students don't see four or five different institutions, 2+2 arrangements, remedial modules, or dual credit options. They simply see themselves involved, learning, and making transitions from one to the other on their way to their goals—their mission. (We're so in to our own missions; students are on a mission; it's their mission that counts.) With relationships, boundaries aren't needed; we move in and out with our students.

There's no need to choose between colleges or even high school or work, we're all right there in the same venue ready with whatever learning, degree, badge, competency, certificate—label it anything because we're good at labeling too. We can talk about a future reality, or we can step back to see a new way and trust we can do it together and just be about starting. My most important job is tending to relationships. I'm so fortunate to have so many, many smart people everywhere around me; they replace partitions with transitions, roles with relationships, boundaries with lots of different paths—none judged lesser. Competition for students has changed to collaboration on everything from shared technology, to shared faculty and staff, to shared employers, to shared students. My most important job is tending to relationships. Fences do not make good neighbors.[67]

Engage Adjunct Faculty with Employers in Teaching and Learning

Community colleges will be first—have been first—in conceiving of employers and working professionals as faculty members. These are the nation's adjunct faculty, already embedded alongside their classically trained academic colleagues. At their best—together—they bring the intersection of professional experience and academic theory, pedagogy and work-based expertise. Because higher education continues to explain away adjunct faculty with an odd embarrassment, institutions haven't fostered this powerful intersection and how it serves students. However, really letting employers into the heart of teaching and learning goes beyond utilizing them as adjunct faculty.

Direct employer and industry involvement will hasten the dissolution of traditional boundaries with higher education, from physical and digital or "digical" mergers to new funding streams to new local, state, and national "edu-econ" models. Less radical may simply be education-based degrees and workplace-based credentials and competencies intertwined in a common setting, not too different from how medical schools and career academies operate today.

Expand the Continuum of Credentials and Who Provides Them

Community colleges, employers, testing agencies, and entire industries are considering new forms of credentials. According to Robert Mundhenk, senior scholar at the Higher Learning Commission, these new representations of what students know and can do upend the notion of completion and even the metrics behind Goal 2025.

As for completion, we need an entirely different metric, probably based on things like student intent. Goal 2025 is fine except it is still too degree-bound, or appears to be. Many students in career programs enroll to get job skills, not degrees, so they leave when they have enough skills to be employable. They may come back in a few years to get a degree, but the priority is employment, and so employment should be a more compelling criterion than graduation, based on student intent and economic realities.[68]

Certificates, diplomas, and degrees comprise the most common credentials in higher education. In the future, these existing credentials may comprise a few in the middle of a much larger continuum that begins with a badge of expertise for a specific skill set (CPR, forklift operation, cash register proficiency, bomb detonation) to something yet to be named, but beyond postdoctoral certificates. Some credentials may be nested, midpoint, or milestones within current degree structures.

The new system would be focused on a person filling up a passport of institution-based and experiential learning, training, and work experience from an early age throughout a full career. What the passport contains is evolving, but badges, certifications, achieved competencies, merits, degrees, diplomas, and stamps are common language around this idea. Whole fields (nursing being one of the most active) are already developing these credentialing models. Agencies, such as the American Nursing Credentialing Center (ANCC), are developing ways of testing and licensing based on them.

Some might declare the continuum a warehouse or an accumulated collection of validated learning acquired by an individual. Others may describe it as learning, training, and experience pathways from initial competencies to integrated disciplinary learning progressions that align with degree frameworks (the five areas of learning in the DQP, for example). These then continue through advanced areas of learning and mastery, including work experience that builds on and goes beyond postdoctoral certificates. Of course, the most radical notion is that traditional higher education maintains authority over some, but not all, of the credentials on the continuum.

John Marr of Cuyahoga Community College asserts that a continuum no longer sidesteps what has remained a dichotomy for community colleges:

> Education, in the minds of many, remains the ticket to a better life, and in this still new millennium, we've called on community colleges like never before to deliver on the promise of the American Dream. The problem is that college degrees for everyone is simply not the answer, and will never

be the answer. We need to embrace our degrees *and* all the non-degree things we do and others do that should still lead to a better life. At the height of the community college movement, Americans still had multiple avenues to reach the middle class, including manufacturing, agriculture, military service, and higher education.

As we have become ever more adept at replacing real workers—and their real wages—with technology solutions and outsourcing, whole categories of honest and necessary work have been thinned right out of our economy. We still need people to weld bridges, construct houses, take care of plumbing, and dispose of hazardous waste. The answer lies in the restoration of a full range of necessary and meaningful work, with preparation provided through high-quality apprenticeships, compulsory education, vocational training programs, and higher education opportunities offered by the systems and institutions best designed to deliver them. With no one type of institution having to shoulder a disproportionate amount of the load, all purveyors of education and workforce training, including community colleges, would have important roles to play.[69]

Apply Translational Research Processes to Higher Education

Translational research in the biomedical sciences—i.e., moving theoretical findings to practical application—is a high priority. The National Institutes of Health offer a model higher education might replicate to translate all the reforms and research results into usable, scalable practices that reach institutions, faculty, and students and are implemented correctly.[70]

Accreditors might serve as data warehouses, working with private foundations and educational organizations to research and translate all the individual pieces of information about institutional practices, reform efforts, day-to-day processes, and policies into clear models of what works and doesn't. Health care has begun to figure out how to scale small clinical victories to full health-care systems within reach of all populations.[71]

Design Based on Bridging Learning Gaps Between Groups

The more that accreditation, state regulations, and federal guidelines shift to "gotcha" mechanisms to flush out unsavory institutions, the less freedom community colleges will have to effectively serve historically disenfranchised populations (e.g., low-income students, first-generation students, and people of color). Maximum time frame, gainful employment, student academic progress, and other ramifications make students who struggle to succeed in community colleges even more difficult to embrace. These students fail, arrive without hope and with stereotypical threats, need six to eight years for an associate degree, need Title IV to live, and need significant and sustained support systems while building academic cultural competence and overcoming the hurdles of belonging in school.

Without enough money to live on, or enough time and freedom to work for that money, many students may never succeed in the current environment, no matter how masterfully teaching and learning are structured. Equity and excellence in the present context requires community colleges, states, the federal government, and accreditors to attend to the basic life needs of students—in other words, to ensure equality of opportunity.

The conversation must shift from concentrating on the problems with educating *these students* to the possibilities of what might be learned from them in order to more effectively serve all students. If persistence to quality employment or to student personal goals could replace persistence to degree and still be Title IV fundable, comprehensive community colleges would enjoy a freedom not talked about since the 1970s. Jeanne Swarthout, president, Northland Pioneer, speaks to the continued need for the open door:

> We serve an astoundingly large region with equally astounding diversity: ethnic, cultural, religious and preparedness. We are a comprehensive community college and will remain so as long as I lead the institution. We are open door. We will remain so. To deny opportunity equally to all who seek our services is not in the definition of comprehensive.[72]

Engage New Forms and Definitions of Learning

Tacit learning is the unwritten, unspoken, vast storehouse of experiential knowledge and skills possessed at some level by all who come through the doors of the community college. In the *New Culture of Learning*, Thomas and Brown speak to the need to make tacit learning visible and documentable as it is in collaborative multi-player role-playing games and simulations, and to put out a call for action to higher education to recognize the need to rethink the ways students expect to learn.

For most of the twentieth century, the explicit was both abundant enough and important enough to sustain an entire system of education practices and institutions that could be sped up and personalized to keep apace with any changes in content. . . . The twenty-first century, however, belongs to the tacit. . . . In a world where things are constantly changing . . . the explicit dimension is no longer a viable model for education.[73]

Tacit learning is a new frontier for community colleges because it is not only about what is learned, but it is about the way it is learned. The implications of accepting the call to action may appear to have a sizable impact on the administration of an institution, but the significance to the faculty may be even greater. Learning outcomes, pedagogy, curricula, and assessment rely on explicit knowledge assessed. Measuring tacit knowledge is a new frontier.

Expand Definitions of Accountability and Its Metrics

To achieve equity and excellence will require sustained effort across higher education, systemic changes, and rethinking what constitutes accountability and quality. Robert Mundhenk emphasizes the level of transparency and honesty about learning that these new definitions may require.

Perhaps institutions might replace or add to the common economic impact report a learning impact report. This instrument could be refined to include not only the placement of graduates, but all job placements. If success is measured in impact rather than graduation rates, the institution's value to the community becomes much more obvious than it seems now. The impact can be much more than economic. Add in programs for seniors, summer programs for kids, etc., and the community college becomes a community resource that potentially has a positive impact on ALL members of the community. That kind of formation probably comes closer to the original ideas behind community colleges when so many were being founded in the 1960s and 1970s, but we don't seem to value or discuss that any longer.[74]

Higher education should applaud the transparency and honesty with which Achieving the Dream leaders have documented both what has and hasn't been successful. Much is learned from a failed hypothesis.

Accountability and quality metrics need measures and methods that credit knowledge gained from all efforts. An expanded definition of accountability would take into account the long view, contextual gains, failed innovations, and contributions to incremental learning about what changes make a difference and eventually lead to the goals. Quality demands metrics and measures that in and of themselves foster equity and excellence.

A new framework for equity and excellence might include measures related to institutional advocacy, student cultural competence and be-longing, time-independent learning, and persistence-to-goal variables. Key performance indicators may shift from absolutes to measures of progression in individual, institutional, community, and societal forma-tion. Failures at innovation should be regarded nearly as highly as suc-cesses, provided the institution uses what it has learned.

ENGAGING THE CONSIDERATIONS AND PROPOSITIONS

McClenney and Mathis remind community college leaders that elevat-ing the student success, equity, learning, and completion agenda will require embedding it into the fabric of the institution and engaging trustees and other college stakeholders in the work.

> Building awareness and understanding of the student learning, equity, success, and completion agenda are critical to foster the political will, involvement, and support needed for long-term engagement in the work. By establishing a shared vision and building a culture in which use of data, evidence, inquiry, and involvement are core, leaders can cultivate an en-vironment in which informed discussions offset hallway conversations and political jockeying; focus on end goals; address calls for accountability; im-prove academic quality, thereby increasing the attainment of educational goals by all students.[75]

Achieving the learning and completion goals requires the long-term work of making up the difference in learning, achievement, and employ-ment gaps of low-income and students of color. The magnitude of the work may cause many to question whether these goals are appropriate, whether it's possible, and how it can be done. Continual questions, cau-tions, and debates on the feasibility of success are a form of filibustering and keeping colleges from acting on what matters.

The answers to "Should we?" and "How is it possible?" are *Yes*. It matters that students learn; learning leads to achievement of individual aspirations, to attainment of credentials, and to fulfillment of individual and societal needs. In *The Answer to How Is Yes,* Peter Block explains that, "'How?'—more than any other question—looks for the answer outside of us." While *how* grasps for techniques and models, *yes* is a commitment to create and test them, to figure it out, to engage, to pursue the vision, to persevere, and to keep acting on what matters anew.[76]

For some, the considerations and propositions strip higher education from what's dearly valued and replaces degrees with lesser forms of attainment and training. Nevertheless, higher education has always placed deep value in the diversity of institutions, autonomy of mission, academic freedom, and liberty to pursue teaching and learning that fulfills its claim for the common good.

These propositions and considerations merely increase this diversity, add to the range of missions, deepen academic freedom, and expand both the forums and means for teaching and learning, as well as who evaluates them, and ways of recognizing them.

No mission or set of purposes is gone. The continuum is both richer and broader. It embraces when learning is for employment and when learning is the end in itself, solely for the expansion of knowledge, appreciation, and culture and never tied to the economy, productivity, the workforce, or even scholarship and research. Essentially, the community college offers fertile ground for innovation to be born, brought to scale, and then expanded into other higher education contexts.

Finally, achieving equity and excellence means not only determining what matters most to do, but also providing enough time to create urgency, a theory, and a vision of what future reality looks like. This means community colleges need (a) to reclaim time to read, ponder, and think; (b) to talk and work together, appreciating what has been, letting go, and creating new designs; and (c) to do these two by convening groups of faculty, staff, students, employers, community members, business leaders—and anyone else willing to commit to reimagining the new culture and patterns of deep learning.

Competency-based education and performance-based authentic assessment of student learning, the focus of the next two chapters, again make plain ways that community colleges continue to commit to student-focused institutions, student-focused teaching, and real determination of what and how well students learn.

The last chapter belongs to those who engage students in the blood and sweat of providing the real and deep learning needed for all they and we aspire to be and do—faculty. Learning matters most. As noted by Cia Verschelden, executive director of institutional assessment at the University of Central Oklahoma, teaching for learning and tending to the moments of every class, not completion, engages faculty. Three hours on Monday night may be the exact point to begin.

> I can't think of a succinct way to state what we all agree is important—the student. I've been a faculty member at a research university, a vice president of academic affairs of a community college, and am now here at a state university. By the standards of my "real job" in assessment, our interest from an institutional perspective is in making confident statements about what OUR STUDENTS know and can do when they graduate with a specific degree. As a teacher and as a chief academic officer on a good day, it's about each STUDENT at a given moment in her or his educational/life journey. It's like the Buddhist teaching that all that matters is now—this minute in this place. My most important work happens in the three hours I spend with students on Monday nights, many of whom have worked all day and have many family responsibilities. This time is precious and has to be spent well. In the life of a student, we can never know what moment on what day and in what place the "magic" will happen, so we need to respect every moment.[77]

Community colleges are the nexus for determining what constitutes an accountable institution, accountable for a student-centered, learning-focused system designed for attainment of valuable fit-to-goal and fit-to-purpose credentials for a nation's and a life's work. By 2025, will community colleges point to a time when education tipped from providing access and pushing completion to sustaining equity—deep learning pathways that bridge racial, economic, social, and other divides—and attending to excellence?

Yes.

It's time to redesign. It's time to act.

How?

The answer to *how* is a commitment to *yes*.[78]

NOTES

1. Alexander K. Mayer et al., *Moving Ahead with Institutional Change: Lessons from the First Round of the Achieving the Dream Community Colleges* (New York: MDRC, Community College Research Center, April 2014), iii, ES–7.

2. U.S. Department of Education, "Meeting the Nation's 2020 Goal: State Targets for Increasing the Number and Percentage of College Graduates with Degrees," March 18, 2011, https://www2.ed.gov/policy/highered/guid/secletter/110323insert.pdf.

3. Alene Russell, "A Guide to Major U.S. College Completion Initiatives" (Washington, D.C.: American Association of State Colleges and Universities, October 2011).

4. Ibid.

5. Anthony P. Carnevale and Jeff Strohl, "How Increasing College Access Is Increasing Inequality and What to Do about It," in *Rewarding Strivers* (New York: Century Foundation Press, 2010), 131–32.

6. Ibid., "Separate and Unequal: How Higher Education Reinforces the Intergenerational Reproduction of White Racial Privilege" (Washington, D.C.: Georgetown Center on Education and the Workforce, 2013), 9.

7. The Report of The Century Foundation Task Force on Preventing Community Colleges from Becoming Separate and Unequal, *Bridging the Higher Education Divide: Strengthening Community Colleges and Restoring the American Dream* (New York: The Century Foundation Press, 2013), 19.

8. Ibid., 5.

9. Thomas G. Mortenson, "Family Income and Educational Attainment 1970 to 2010," *Postsecondary Education Opportunity* 235 (January 2012).

10. Ibid., "Family Income and Educational Attainment 1970 to 2009," *Postsecondary Education Opportunity* 221 (November 2010).

11. Anthony P. Carnevale and Jeff Strohl, *Separate and Unequal: How Higher Education Reinforces the Intergenerational Reproduction of White Racial Privilege* (Washington, D.C.: The Georgetown University Center on Education and the Workforce, 2013), 11.

12. The Pell Institute for the Study of Opportunity in Higher Education, *Developing 20/20 Vision on the 2020 Degree Attainment Goal: The Threat of Income-Based Inequality in Education* (Washington, D.C.: Council for Opportunity in Education, May 2011).

13. OECD, *Education at a Glance 2014: OECD Indicators* (OECD Publishing, September 2014).

14. John E. Roueche, George A. Baker III, and Richard L. Brownell, *Accountability and the Community College: Direction for the '70s* (Washington, D.C.: American Association of Community and Junior Colleges, 1972).

15. Carol P. Thompson, Richard L. Alfred, and Malcolm Lowther, "Institutional Effort: A Reality-Based Model for Assessment of Community College Productivity," *Community College Review* 15, no. 2 (1987): 28–37.

16. James L. Hudgins, "Institutional Effectiveness: A Strategy for Institutional Renewal," *Occasional Paper* 9, no. 1 (Atlanta: Southern Association of Community and Technical Colleges, 1991).

17. Community College Roundtable, *Community Colleges: Core Indicators of Effectiveness* (Washington, D.C.: American Association of Community Colleges, 1994).

18. John E. Roueche, Laurence F. Johnson, Suanne D. Roueche, and Associates, *Embracing the Tiger: The Effectiveness Debate and the Community College* (Washington, D.C.: Community College Press/American Association of Community Colleges, 1997).

19. Ibid.

20. John E. Roueche, Barton R. Herrscher, and George A. Baker III, "Time as the Variable, Achievement as the Constant: Competency-Based Education Instruction in the Community College," *Horizons Monograph Series* (Washington, D.C.: American Association of Community Colleges, 1976).

21. Academic Quality Improvement Program (AQIP), Higher Learning Commission, http://ncahlc.org/Pathways/aqip-home.html.

22. Academic Quality Improvement Program (AQIP), "Action Project Directory," Higher Learning Commission, http://www.ncahlc.org/component/com_apdsearch/Itemid,126/.

23. Center for Community College Student Engagement (CCCSE), *A Matter of Degrees: Practices to Pathways, High-Impact Practices for Community College Success* (Austin, TX: The University of Texas at Austin, Program in Higher Education Leadership, 2014).

24. Alexander K. Mayer et al., *Moving Ahead with Institutional Change: Lessons from the First Round of the Achieving the Dream Community Colleges* (New York: MDRC, Community College Research Center, April 2014), ix.

25. Ibid.

26. David Moltz, "Dream On," *Inside Higher Ed*, February 10, 2011, https://www.insidehighered.com/news/2011/02/10/five_years_of_achieving_the_dream_in_community_colleges?width=775&height=500&iframe=true.

27. Center for Community College Student Engagement (CCCSE), *A Matter of Degrees: Practices to Pathways, High-Impact Practices for Community College Success* (Austin, TX: The University of Texas at Austin, Program in Higher Education Leadership, 2014), 3.

28. Sanford C. Shugart, "Rethinking the Completion Agenda," in *The Completion Agenda*, ed. the editors of Inside Higher Ed (Washington, D.C.: Inside Higher Ed, 2014), 20.

29. Roberta Teahen (Associate Provost, Ferris State University), e-mail message to author, September 14, 2014.

30. Margaretta Brédé Mathis, "Perspectives: Adapting to Achieve," *Diverse Issues in Higher Education,* February 26, 2010. http://diverseeducation.com/article/13575/.

31. Center for Community College Student Engagement (CCCSE), *A Matter of Degrees: Practices to Pathways, High-Impact Practices for Community College Success* (Austin, TX: The University of Texas at Austin, Program in Higher Education Leadership, 2014), 34–35; Alexander K. Mayer, Oscar Cerna, Dan Cullinan, Kelley Fong, Elizabeth Zachry Rutschow, and Davis Jenkins, *Moving Ahead with Institutional Change: Lessons from the First Round of the Achieving the Dream Community Colleges* (New York: MDRC, Community College Research Center, April 2014), 42–46; Davis Jenkins, "Redesigning Community Colleges for Completion: Lessons from Research on High-Performance Organizations," Community College Research Center, Working Paper No. 21. (New York: Community College Research Center, 2011); Adrianna Kezar, "What Is the Best Way to Achieve Broader Reach of Improved Practices in Higher Education?" Innovative Higher Education 36, no. 4 (2011): 235–47.

32. The Pell Institute for the Study of Opportunity in Higher Education, *Developing 20/20 Vision on the 2020 Degree Attainment Goal: The Threat of Income-Based Inequality in Education* (Washington, D.C.: Council for Opportunity in Education, May 2011).

33. Sanford C.5, "Rethinking the Completion Agenda," in *The Completion Agenda*, ed. the editors of Inside Higher Ed (Washington, D.C.: Inside Higher Ed, 2014), 20.

34. Peter T. Ewell, ed., *U.S. Accreditation and the Future of Quality Assurance* (Washington, D.C.: Council for Higher Education Accreditation, 2008).

33. Paul Gaston, *Higher Education Accreditation: How It's Changing and Why It Must* (Sterling, VA: Stylus Publishing, 2013).

36. U.S. Department of Education, Office of the Assistant Secretary, Dear Colleague Letter, "Guidance to Institutions and Accrediting Agencies Regarding a Credit Hour as Defined in the Final Regulations Published on October 29, 2010," GEN-11-06 (Washington, D.C., March 18, 2011).

37. Edvard Munch, *The Scream*, 1895. The case example is drawn from the author's experience overseeing the Higher Learning Commission's substantive change processes that require institutions, per federal regulation, to seek approval for contractual arrangements with non-accredited entities.

38. Margaret Spellings, secretary of education, "A Test of Leadership: Charting the Future of U.S. Higher Education," Report of the Commission

on the Future of Higher Education (Washington, D.C.: U.S. Department of Education, 2006).

39. Nancy B. Shulock, ed., *Practitioners on Making Accountability Work for the Public*, New Directions for Higher Education, no. 135 (San Francisco: Jossey-Bass, 2006).

40. A Report of the ACE National Task Force on Institutional Accreditation, *Assuring Academic Quality in the 21st Century: Self-Regulation in a New Era* (Washington, D.C.: American Council on Education, April 2012).

41. Ibid.

42. The Higher Learning Commission, "Documenting Fundamental Understandings: Minimum Expectations in the Criteria" (Chicago, IL: The Higher Learning Commission, July 30, 2010).

43. U.S. Department of Education, "Department of Education Establishes New Student Aid Rules to Protect Borrowers and Taxpayers" (Washington, D.C.: U.S. Department of Education, October 28, 2010).

44. A Report of the ACE National Task Force on Institutional Accreditation, *Assuring Academic Quality in the 21st Century: Self-Regulation in a New Era* (Washington, D.C.: American Council on Education, April 2012), 17.

45. U.S. Department of Education, "Department of Education Releases List of Higher Education Institutions with Open Title IX Sexual Violence Investigations" (Washington, D.C.: U.S. Department of Education, May 1, 2014).

46. Anya Kamenetz and John O'Connor, "The Collapse of Corinthian Colleges," *National Public Radio*, July 8, 2014.

47. Andrew Roth, "Musings on the Future of Higher Ed: The Worst of Times," *The Evolution*, September 22, 2014, http://www.evolllution.com/opinions/musings-future-higher-ed-worst times/?utm_source=newsletter&utm_medium=email&utm_campaign=sep22.

48. Jeanne Swarthout (President, Northland Pioneer College), e-mail message to author, August 13, 2014.

49. George Boggs, "Through the Learning Lens," in *The Completion Agenda*, ed. the editors of Inside Higher Ed (Washington, D.C.: Inside Higher Ed, 2014), 27–28.

50. Linda Darling-Hammond, "Race, Inequality, and Educational Inequality: The Irony of No Child Left Behind," *Race, Ethnicity, and Education* 10, no. 3 (2007): 246.

51. Center for Community College Student Engagement (CCCSE), *A Matter of Degrees: Practices to Pathways, High-Impact Practices for Community College Success* (Austin, TX: The University of Texas at Austin, Program in Higher Education Leadership, 2014), 34.

52. The Report of The Century Foundation Task Force on Preventing Community Colleges from Becoming Separate and Unequal, *Bridging the Higher Education Divide: Strengthening Community Colleges and Restoring the American Dream* (New York: The Century Foundation Press, 2013), 6.

53. Ibid., 4.

54. Jennifer Engle and Colleen O'Brien, *Demography Is Not Destiny: Increasing the Graduation Rates of Low-Income Students at Large Public Universities* (Washington, D.C.: The Pell Institute, 2007), 6.

55. Margaret J. Wheatley, *Finding Our Way: Leadership for an Uncertain Time* (San Francisco: Berrett-Koehler, 2007), 136.

56. Jonathan Keiser (associate vice chancellor, City Colleges of Chicago), in discussion with author, August 28, 2014.

57. David H. Kalsbeek, "The 4Ps as a Guiding Perspective," in *Reframing Retention Strategy for Institutional Improvement*, ed. David H. Kalsbeek, *New Directions for Higher Education*, no. 161 (San Francisco: Jossey-Bass, Spring 2013), 102.

58. Center for Community College Student Engagement (CCCSE), *A Matter of Degrees: Practices to Pathways, High-Impact Practices for Community College Success* (Austin, TX: The University of Texas at Austin, Program in Higher Education Leadership, 2014), 2.

59. Daniel H. Kim, *Organizing for Learning; Strategies for Knowledge Creation and Enduring Change* (Waltham, MA: Pegasus Communications, Inc., 2001), 59–67.

60. Jeff Selingo, "Reimagining the Undergraduate Experience: 4 Provocative Ideas," *The Chronicle of Higher Education*, June 22, 2014.

61. Margaret J. Wheatley, *Finding Our Way: Leadership for an Uncertain Time* (San Francisco: Berrett-Koehler, 2007), 215.

62. The Report of The Century Foundation Task Force on Preventing Community Colleges from Becoming Separate and Unequal, *Bridging the Higher Education Divide: Strengthening Community Colleges and Restoring the American Dream* (New York: The Century Foundation Press, 2013).

63. Dennis P. Jones, *Outcomes-Based Funding: The Wave of Implementation* (Boulder, CO: NCHEMS, Complete College America, 2013).

64. Alexander K. Mayer et al., *Moving Ahead with Institutional Change: Lessons from the First Round of the Achieving the Dream Community Colleges* (New York: MDRC, Community College Research Center, April 2014).

65. Robert Mundhenk (senior scholar, The Higher Learning Commission; former chief academic officer, Northampton County Area Community College), e-mail message to author, August 10, 2014.

66. Robert Frost, "Mending Wall," ed. Louis Untermeyer, *Modern American Poetry* (New York: Harcourt, Brace, and Howe, 1919; Bartleby.com 1999), www.bartleby.com/104/, lines 34–35.

67. Michael Chipps (president, Northeast Community College, NE) in discussion with author, August 20, 2014.

68. Robert Mundhenk (senior scholar, The Higher Learning Commission; former chief academic officer, Northampton County Area Community College), e-mail message to author, August 10, 2014.

69. John W. Marr Jr. (dean of academic affairs, Cuyahoga Community College, Eastern Campus), in discussion with the author, August 17, 2014.

70. Steven H. Woolf, "The Meaning of Translational Research and Why It Matters," *JAMA* 299, no. 2 (2008): 211–13.

71. Ibid.

72. Jeanne Swarthout (president, Northland Pioneer College), e-mail message to author, August 13, 2014.

73. Douglas Thomas and John Seely Brown, *A New Culture of Learning: Cultivating the Imagination for a World of Constant Change* (Lexington, KY: Douglas Thomas and John Seely Brown, 2011), 76.

74. Robert Mundhenk (senior scholar, The Higher Learning Commission; former chief academic officer, Northampton County Area Community College), e-mail message to author, August 10, 2014.

75. Byron McClenney and Martha Mathis, *Making Good on the Promise of the Open Door: Effective Governance and Leadership to Improve Student Equity, Success, and Completion* (Washington, D.C.: Association of Community College Trustees, 2011), 33.

76. Peter Block, *The Answer to How Is Yes: Acting on What Matters* (San Francisco: Berrett-Koehler Publishers, Inc., 2002), 1.

77. Cia Verschelden (executive director of institutional assessment at University of Central Oklahoma; former VPAA at Highland Community College, KS), in discussion with author, August 14, 2014.

78. Peter Block, *The Answer to How Is Yes: Acting on What Matters* (San Francisco: Berrett-Koehler Publishers, Inc., 2002).

3

COMPETENCY-BASED EDUCATION

Laurie Dodge

A new model of competency-based education is emerging through-out the nation at colleges and universities that are student-centered and concerned with current and future U.S. workforce needs. This new model addresses the "iron triangle" of simultaneously containing costs, enhancing quality, and expanding access to serve more students of all backgrounds. Community colleges are well poised to develop this new model of competency-based education (CBE) programs based on their strong community roots, partnerships with employers, alignment of curriculum with industry standards, and commitment to student success.

This chapter provides a brief overview of the history, and the definitions and design, of competency-based education. Then it presents illustrative case studies of three community colleges and systems-guided pathways to consider for developing cutting edge competency-based education programs that not only address the "iron triangle" but move well beyond it to produce more graduates with high-quality, high-value postsecondary degrees and credentials.

REEMERGENCE OF COMPETENCY-BASED EDUCATION

Why is a new model of competency-based education emerging at this time? First and foremost, there is a national call to action. President Obama in his State of the Union Address on February 12, 2013, called for a performance-based financial aid system. Over $150 billion is spent on direct loan and grant aid for students each year. "The President called on Congress to consider value, affordability, and student outcomes in making determinations about which colleges and universities receive access to federal student aid."[1] Because of limited resources and other considerations (e.g., performance funding), it is imperative that community colleges be strategic in implementing new initiatives to meet the president's call to action for an additional five million graduates from community colleges by 2020.

This call to action for a new model of competency-based education also addresses the economic and workforce needs by providing workers with twenty-first-century competencies. Anthony P. Carnevale, director of the Georgetown University Center on Education and the Workforce, reviewed the recently completed Occupational Net (O*NET) database that specifies the set of occupational competencies required for success in particular occupations and related careers.

Carnevale found that twenty-first-century skills are the competencies required for jobs in the future. The top knowledge, skills, and abilities (KSAs) required across most occupations include active listening, speaking, critical thinking, reading comprehension, oral comprehension and expression, written comprehension, and problem sensitivity. In addition, key competencies for the future workforce include work values, work interest, and personal qualities.[2] The KSAs frame what the future workforce will need and what graduates must learn and achieve while obtaining their higher education credentials.

Second, technology is a major factor in the development of a new model of competency-based education. Technology greatly influences how students learn and how faculty deliver curriculum. Students are seeking convenience in achieving their educational goals, leading some to suppose that 60 percent of students will be taking classes entirely online by 2020.[3]

Trend data supports this movement to online delivery, as evidenced by the annual increase of 2.5 percent for the average higher education student body compared to the annual increase of online learning of 16.1 percent.[4] This data supports that the majority of growth is in online education.

Technology also influences teaching and learning through utilization of data analytics, gamification, simulations, and adaptive learning. These powerful technological tools adapt to accommodate students' preferred learning modalities and provide evidence of acquired knowledge. Through technology, students are provided with a more personalized approach and greater access to achieving higher education credentials.

A third influence for competency-based education is the *new student*, also known as the New Majority. National trends continue to push on the definition of a typical college student. Currently, only 14 percent of all undergraduates attend full-time and live on campus.[5] Student demographics are also changing significantly. The National Center for Education Statistics (2013) report titled "Projections of Education Statistics through 2021" predicted growth from 2010 to 2021, suggesting significant differences in ethnicity, age, gender, and part-time status in the next decade. Growth for Hispanics over this eleven-year period is 43 percent, and for blacks the growth rate is predicted at 25 percent.

By comparison, the predicted growth for whites is a mere 4 percent. Growth in older students is also predicted with growth rates for younger students, ages eighteen to twenty-four, at 10 percent while the growth rate for twenty-five- to thirty-four-year-olds is 20 percent, and for those older than thirty-five the growth rate is predicted at 25 percent. In addition, more women are predicted to attend college (18 percent versus 10 percent for men), and more students will be attending college on a part-time basis (18 percent versus 14 percent for full-time).

Fourth, employers are voicing (and being heard) regarding what graduates need to know and be able to do to be prepared for the workforce. Hart Research Associates (2013) conducted a survey on behalf of the Association of American Colleges and Universities (AAC&U) to ask employers what they are looking for in ready-to-work graduates.[6] Nearly all employers (95 percent) say they give hiring preference to college graduates with skills that enable them to contribute to innovation in the workplace.

Employers recognize that necessary skills for success in careers cut across majors, and over 90 percent of the employers want graduates who (1) can think critically, (2) can communicate clearly, (3) can solve complex problems, (4) can demonstrate ethical judgment and integrity, (5) possess intercultural skills, and (6) have the capacity for continued new learning. It is evident that employers want graduates with twenty-first-century skills. Are colleges meeting the needs of employers? Hart found that only 56 percent of employers expressed satisfaction with the efforts of colleges and universities to prepare graduates for success in the workplace.

In summary, these forces and influences from the national call to action by President Obama and other stakeholders, to the expedient pace of technology changes in education, to a new majority student, and finally to employers voicing the necessary knowledge, skills, and abilities that students need to be successful in the workplace, have collectively set fertile ground for a new model of competency-based education. It is within this context and setting that community colleges can and are creating relevant, quality, affordable, and accessible competency-based education programs.

HISTORY OF COMPETENCY-BASED EDUCATION

The geneses of competency-based education programs in the United States were in the 1970s.[7] These pioneer institutions used a competency framework (e.g., broad learning outcomes or areas of study) for defining their degrees. Competency-based programs were viewed as a viable option for adult learners who were entering college with knowledge, experience, and skills that would allow them to progress through college at a faster rate.

The first competency-based programs were developed using student learning outcomes (competencies) as a framework for degree completion and/or prior learning options such as home-grown final challenge examinations, standardized tests (e.g., College-Level Examination Program [CLEP], DSST Exams), and credit for prior learning (e.g., portfolio, and military and corporate training and coursework evaluated by the American Council on Education). The first competency-based programs were few in number for the first twenty years in the United States.

A few pioneer institutions in the 1970s paved the way for the next wave in competency-based education. In the mid-1990s, Western Governors University (WGU) created a new university, in which all programs were competency-based. Built by the governors of nineteen western states, WGU addressed both the employer's need for graduates to possess work-ready abilities and the student's need to reduce the cost of a college credential. Each degree program at WGU has defined competencies written by industry professionals and subject matter experts.

Students at WGU take assessments to test mastery of required competencies. Faculty members work with students to determine their learning activities to prepare for the assessments. Students can progress at their own pace, though a minimal progression must be met to comply with financial aid regulations. In addition, each competency is mapped back to a credit-hour course to assist in transfer, transcripts, and financial aid.

WGU now enrolls approximately 39,000 students and has awarded over 23,000 credentials in teacher education, business, information technology, and health professions. WGU exponentially and positively influenced the movement of competency-based education by providing industry-related competencies, requiring mastery of competencies through assessments, and permitting students to work at their own pace.

Interestingly, although WGU had the option of being the first institution to use the Department of Education Direct Assessment option for financial aid, they chose not to. This Direct Assessment provision was created for WGU, and currently, any college can apply for Direct Assessment for their competency-based education programs.

The Direct Assessment provision in the Higher Education Act allows financial aid to be made available to students in a program that "in lieu of credit hours or clock hours as the measure of student learning, utilizes direct assessment of student learning."[8] The distinction between financial aid via direct assessment and financial aid for credit-based programs requires some clarification. For credit-based programs, financial aid is provided to students based on time (e.g., semester). In a direct assessment program, students are provided with financial aid based on successful completion of competencies (not time-based).

In sum, over this twenty-year period, one can see the start-up and then the next generation of competency-based education. The 1970s brought creative solutions and new approaches to degree and credential completion by providing frameworks of learning outcomes (competencies) and opportunities for students to acquire college credit through examination, prior learning, and training.

The mid-1990s brought a new university (WGU) whose university-wide competency-based education approach reflected relevant and affordable self-paced programs and focus on mastery through assessments. These significant historical events have led us to the emergence of a new model of competency-based education. To explain the new competency-based education model, a review of definitions and components is appropriate.

Definitions and Design of Competency-Based Education Programs

If asking what differentiates competency-based education from traditional higher education, one would likely hear that, as opposed to traditional models, learning is constant and time varies for competency-based education. And, of course, the traditional approach to higher education is based on the credit hour, where time is inviolate.

Completion of a bachelor's degree typically requires 120 credits, including courses in general education, a chosen major area of study, and electives. In the traditional approach, time is constant with discrete beginning and ending times for learning activities (e.g., 3-credit course = 45 hours of instruction + assignments over a semester of 15 weeks). However, learning varies as students complete courses with varying levels of mastery and knowledge.

Amy Laitinen, in her seminal piece, *Cracking the Credit Hour*, describes the origin of the credit hour. Carnegie developed a system to compensate faculty during retirement, a free pension system for professors, run by the Carnegie Foundation for the Advancement of Teaching. The foundation promoted high school reform by requiring that any college wishing to participate in the pension plan had to use the "standard unit" (aka, the Carnegie Unit) for high school graduation and college admissions purposes. Thereby, the Carnegie Unit was used for colleges to convert their areas of study into time-based units, serving as workload measures for faculty as well as requirements for student graduation and degree completion.[9]

Definitions

Competency-based education requires students to demonstrate mastery of specific learning outcomes through assessment. Although a more precise and widely accepted taxonomy would be helpful in communicating what competency-based is and is not, definitions of CBE are highly discussed, and still a work in progress. Following are some definitions by leading organizations and agencies focusing on competency-based education:

- EDUCAUSE—The competency-based education (CBE) approach allows students to advance based on their ability to master a skill or competency at their own pace regardless of environment. This method is tailored to meet different learning abilities and can lead to more efficient student outcomes.[10]
- The Council for Adult and Experiential Learning (CAEL)— Competency-based degree programs focus more on what students learn, rather than where or how long the learning takes place. Instead of evaluating student progress on the amount of time spent in a classroom (using the credit hour, which is the default standard for measuring progress), students receive college credit based on their actual demonstration of skills learned.[11]
- Competency-Based Education Network (C-BEN)—Competency-based education is a flexible way for students to get credit for what they know, build on their knowledge and skills by learning more at their own pace, and earn high-quality degrees, certificates, and other credentials that help them in their lives and careers. Students in these programs show what they know and how well they know it through multiple ways of evaluating learning. This is another choice for learning offered at many institutions, through a variety of programs, with full support to help students when needed.[12]
- American Council on Education (ACE) and Blackboard— Competency-based education (CBE) is an alternative to the credit hour–based system of credentialing. Student progress is based on demonstration of proficiency and/or mastery as measured through

assessments and/or through application of credit for prior learning. In competency-based education programs, time is the variable and student competency mastery is the focus, rather than a fixed-time model where students achieve varying results. In competency-based education, as distinct from competency-based learning, the focus is on academic programs, practices, and policies.[13]

In the Degree Qualifications Profile, posted October 1, 2014, a competency-based degree was defined as "an academic credential awarded for demonstrated competency rather than for the accumulation of credit hours through taking course."[14] In contrast to "competency," the authors described "proficiency" as students' mastery reflecting more than being competent or adequate and that a higher bar of attainment was necessary to demonstrate capacity for further learning. This higher bar or proficiency was defined as "a label for a set of demonstrations of knowledge, understanding and skill that satisfy the levels of mastery sufficient to justify the award of an academic degree."[15]

For a competency-based demonstration project, the House of Representatives stated:

> the term "competency-based education" means an educational process that (A) is characterized by the measurement of learning as opposed to the measurement of instructional and learning time; and (B) includes direct measures of learning, which may include projects, papers, examinations, presentations, performances, and portfolios, and direct measures by others of student learning, in place of, or in addition to, using credit hours or clock hours to measure learning.[16]

Although these definitions provide a basic understanding of what competency-based education is, they still vary. This lack of a universal lexicon creates problems when differentiating what is and is not competency-based education. It is problematic in terms of quality standards and transferability.[17]

This new wave in competency-based education is still emerging, and ambiguity exists, as evidenced in the various definitions. Assessment strategies in building tools and determining how a student will demonstrate mastery of a competency is the heart of a competency-based education program. And a framework or common characteristics of competency-based education is a step toward a more universal understanding of CBE. Based on the previously cited definitions, guidelines for a competency-based education could be described as:

1. Mastery of learning is the focus and not time.
2. Competencies are explicit, measureable, relevant, and applicable learning outcomes.
3. Assessment is rigorous, reliable, and valid.

Program Design

With this basic understanding of the definition of competency-based education, it is helpful to describe how a competency-based program is constructed. The approach to designing and building a competency-based program sets the foundation for the student learning journey and methods for assessment.

Deconstruction-Reconstruction

A common approach for institutions is the Deconstruction-Reconstruction approach. This approach focuses on current curricula and programs, specifically program-level learning outcomes and course-level learning outcomes. Faculty deconstruct, or take apart, an existing degree program outcome by outcome for each course. These "bite-sized" outcomes are normally course outcomes that are then reorganized into new categories. These new categories or groupings of outcomes change the framework of a degree or specific required courses to a group of competencies. Following are basic steps to illustrate the Deconstruction-Reconstruction approach:

Step One—For each course required in a degree program, collect each course learning outcome.

Step Two—Code each course learning outcome to track its original source (e.g., course discipline and course number).

Step Three—Write each outcome separately. Each outcome now "lives" on its own.

Step Four—Categorize each outcome (e.g., oral communication, analytical thinking, applied learning, etc.).

Step Five—Write an overarching competency statement that addresses all of the individual outcomes. Note that sometimes one of the outcomes in the group may serve as the overarching outcome.

Step Six—Ensure alignment of the individual outcomes in this category, making revisions to statements for clarity, measurability, and appropriate level of learning.

Step Seven—This new grouping of outcomes (e.g., overarching competency statement and relevant objectives) is now the new competency.

To illustrate the Deconstruction-Reconstruction approach, in Table 3.1 is an example from Brandman University's COMU 101 Public Speaking credit-hour course and the equivalent Oral Communication competency. For the Public Speaking course, the course description and course learning outcomes are listed. For the Oral Communication competency, the overarching competency statement and competency objectives are listed.

The Deconstruction-Reconstruction approach is much like taking a building apart piece by piece and making a new structure by using most of the same pieces, though one can get rid of redundant pieces and add new pieces based on stakeholder input. This new structure may be more streamlined, efficient, and effective, with scaffolding of learning outcomes and orchestrated "connect the dots" learning threaded throughout the educational journey.

Framework Origin

In addition to the Deconstruction-Reconstruction model for curriculum development, an institution may wish to start with a Framework Origin approach. The American Association of Colleges and Universities (AAC&U) developed the Liberal Education and America's Promise (LEAP) Essential Learning Outcomes.[18] For students to prepare for twenty-first-century challenges, outcome statements were written for the following categories: (1) Knowledge of Human Cultures and the Physical and Natural World; (2) Intellectual and Practical Skills; (3) Personal and Social Responsibility; and (4) Integrative and Applied Learning. AAC&U continued this good work further by creating rubrics for assessing outcomes in each of these areas.[19]

Another framework for curriculum development is the Degree Qualifications Profile (DQP). Commissioned by Lumina Foundation, it outlines what all college students should know and be able to do at the associate, bachelor's, and master's level to prepare for twenty-first-century workforce needs: (1) Specialized Knowledge; (2) Broad and Integrative Knowledge;

Table 3.1. Oral Communication Credit-Hour Course & Competency.

COMU 101 Public Speaking

The primary goal of COMU 101 is to provide students with the opportunity to improve their public speaking skills in the areas of preparation and delivery. The method of speaking emphasized is extemporaneous. Though public speaking is the primary focus of the course, other issues of communication, such as written, interpersonal, and group, are also discussed. In addition, students will learn to be more critical consumers of communication.

Oral Communication Competency: Deliver a well-organized presentation using delivery techniques and supporting materials appropriate for the audience.

Course Learning Outcomes:

1. Demonstrate an understanding of the elements and the transactional nature of communication.
2. Recognize and accept causes of perceptual differences.
3. Demonstrate an understanding of the communication process through invention, organization, drafting, revision, editing, and presentation.
4. Demonstrate use of improved listening skills.
5. Demonstrate basic patterns used in public speaking—composition, organization, and audience analysis.
6. Effectively interact in group activities, discussions, and presentations.
7. Speak clearly, accurately, and fluently with a sense of continuity.
8. Prepare and deliver a variety of speeches that effectively inform, persuade, and commemorate.
9. Construct speech outlines incorporating a thesis statement and specific purpose.
10. Effectively use research and other supporting material to back up claims orally and in writing.
11. Differentiate between verbal and nonverbal symbols in various levels of communication and develop effective use of space, body language, gestures, eye contact, vocal emphasis, modulation, and pacing.

Competency Objectives:

1. Understand the foundational elements of oral communication.
2. Apply audience analysis to the formulation and execution of an oral presentation.
3. Identify and support central ideas that are demonstrated in a topic selection, a full-sentence outline, a speaking outline, an oral presentation, and a reference list.
4. Create an effective oral presentation that includes an introduction, body, and conclusion that are evident in a full sentence outline, a speaking outline, and an oral presentation.
5. Demonstrate the ability to speak confidently and use verbal and nonverbal communication effectively in an oral presentation.
6. Apply effective delivery strategies, including the use of notes and presentation aids, to the performance of an oral presentation.

(Brandman University 2015).

(3) Intellectual Skills; (4) Applied and Collaborative Learning; and (5) Civic and Global Learning. The DQP is used frequently as a framework in undergraduate competency-based education programs.[20] For example, Brandman University and Southern New Hampshire University use it as a framework for their competency-based education programs.

Some colleges choose a framework that is based on industry standards. This approach is an effective means for programs that are tightly aligned to existing professional standards. To address the knowledge, skills, and abilities necessary for a discipline or targeted profession, there are industry-specific databases, such as the U.S. Department of Labor/Employment and Training Administration's Occupational Information Network (O*NET) database, that list hundreds of occupational definitions and learning outcomes associated with specific jobs. In addition, many professions (e.g., nurses, counselors, teachers, engineers) outline specific standards and outcomes for which students must demonstrate competency.[21]

The Framework Origin approach differs from the Deconstruction-Reconstruction approach in that the Framework approach builds on an existing, predefined notion of a credential while Reconstruction rebuilds credentials from outcomes in existing courses.

The Framework approach permits a true fresh palette to building a degree program. Once competencies have been established through the Framework Origin approach, the next important step is to conduct a gap analysis by asking relevant stakeholders (e.g., alumni, employers, and subject matter experts) what knowledge, skills, and abilities are missing.

The careful analysis of the competencies required for a credential not only provides a transparent understanding of the meaning of the degree but also provides the opportunity of tuning of credentials as described in chapter 5. Common questions asked of prospective employers are "Would you hire a graduate of this CBE program? Why or why not? What are missing knowledge, skills, and abilities?" In addition, institutions can also fill in gaps of mission-driven outcomes necessary for all of their graduates.

Traditional or Backward Design

Whether an institution chooses a Deconstruction-Reconstruction approach or a Framework Origin approach in defining the competencies for a credential, once they have identified a framework for defining competencies, they are ready for the next step of designing the assessments and educational activities.

This next step can be conducted in a Traditional or Backward Design approach. Competency statements and supporting objectives provide the structure of the competency-based education program. An institution will then need to determine the educational activities and the assessments that attend to the competencies. The sequence of these two next steps may vary with either curriculum development as a second step (Traditional Approach) or assessment building as a second step (Backward Design).

Traditional Approach	Backward Design
1. Write Competency Statements	1. Write Competency Statements
2. Develop Curriculum Activities	2. *Build Assessments*
3. *Build Assessments*	3. Develop Curriculum Activities

The difference in the approaches is the emphasis on the assessment in the Backward Design. The Backward Design approach supports a clear alignment of the curriculum activities to what is assessed, ensuring a successful pathway for students to demonstrate mastery of the competency. The Traditional Approach focuses on the curriculum as step two, building learning activities and materials first and then composing a means for assessing student learning. This Traditional Approach is much like what most faculty have used in preparing and delivering courses. Normally the book, learning activities, and assignments are prepared before the examinations and assessments are developed.

In Backward Design, the assessment tool is developed prior to creating the learning activities. An assessment blueprint is developed, targeting the specific objectives in each competency. An assessment method is selected (e.g., objective-based or performance-based). Each of the objectives (and in some cases sub-objectives) is assigned a relative weight in the assessment. For example, in a performance-based assessment of writing a research paper, grammar may carry a lower weight than theory. Performance-based assessments are evaluated using a rubric, whereas objective-based assessments are evaluated using tools such as multiple-choice, matching, and closed-choice fill-in-the-blank. An assessment blueprint targeting specific outcomes and weights (e.g., number or items) is also developed for objective assessments.

Choosing the Backward Design versus Traditional approach is an important consideration. Because competency-based education sets the scene for a new approach to teaching and learning, the Backward Design permits several advantages:

1. From the beginning there is a strong framework (e.g., students can answer, "what are the five to ten things I must know, be able to do, and demonstrate to achieve mastery on this competency?").
2. The learning journey and educational activities are clearly aligned to the competency outcome, reducing extraneous and irrelevant content.
3. The learning is intentional and scaffolds within each competency building toward mastery.
4. Carefully constructed formative assessment can be built in each competency aligned with each sub-goal of a competency building. Formative assessment permits adaptive learning (e.g., students show mastery of some content areas and are directed to less-known areas for continued study).
5. Keeping the end in mind (final summative assessment) helps to establish what students need to know and the best pathway for achievement. This keeps student-centered learning as the guiding light in building educational journeys.

Program Components

Earlier in this chapter, after reviewing various definitions of competency-based education, the following common elements were noted:

1. Mastery of learning is the focus and not time.
2. Competencies are explicit, measureable, relevant, and applicable learning outcomes.
3. Assessment is rigorous, reliable, and valid.

Based on the exploration of how competency-based education programs are developed through a Deconstruction-Reconstruction or a Framework Origin model, the following program components of a CBE can be added to the list of elements:

4. The educational journey is intentional, aligning learning opportunities and activities with pertinent knowledge, skills, abilities, and behaviors.
5. The approach is student-centered, creating a clear, transparent pathway to achievement and success.
6. The curriculum reflects relevant knowledge, skills, and abilities.
7. The learning is designed to scaffold from lower levels (e.g., understand, know) to higher levels (e.g., evaluate, apply).

Approaches and Models of Competency-Based Education: Three Case Studies

To help illustrate the approaches to competency-based education (CBE) described in this chapter, three community colleges were solicited as case studies. Each college was in the process of developing or offering a CBE program with some institutions further down the road in their development and implementation, while others were in the beginning stages. They all were taking a comprehensive approach to building their CBE programs by incorporating many of the steps and elements described earlier. Each case study highlights the delivery model, program design, and approach to assessment.

Broward College

Annie Myers, district director for the college's U.S. Department of Labor Trade Adjustment Assistance Community College and Career Training (TAACCCT) grant and professor at Broward College, described their CBE program as a TAACCCT-funded program offering three fully online and hybrid (online courses with optional weekly meeting or individual student support) programs. Broward's CBE work is with the following credentials: (1) Associate of Science Degree in Computer Systems Specialist; (2) Technical Certificate in Information Technology Support Specialist; and (3) Technical Certificate in Information Technology.[22]

Program Design
Broward College began with existing, traditional face-to-face programs, mapping outcomes to competencies, and then mapping competencies

to learning objectives using the Deconstruction-Reconstruction approach previously described in this chapter. Through the grant, Broward received training and resources in curriculum development and assessment development adapted from WGU's model. A standardized online template was used to build all competencies that included open-source and original content. Each course also included a Pace Chart, which recommends the amount of time it should take to complete the course, with options for slower or quicker paces.

The course development process for the CBE courses was similar to development of traditional courses but with the major changes in consistency of the course template and separation of course and assessment developers. Broward College followed a five-step curriculum development process to adapt the existing face-to-face courses to a CBE delivery model.

1. Program-level competencies were identified and defined. Program-level competencies were drawn from the Florida Department of Education, aligning with state standards.
2. The content and assessment development teams were selected by the deans. Each team was composed of one to two faculty content developers and one assessment developer.
3. The course outlines and learning objectives were reviewed to ensure common understanding of the learning objectives.
4. The course was created in the online template with assistance from an instructional technologist.
5. Quality assurance was conducted to assess courses using a specified rubric.

Assessment

Assessments were developed based on the type of course. Technology-rich courses that had labs or other hands-on components had objective and project-based elements. The majority of assessments were faculty developed. Industry certifications also served as assessments, when appropriate. Each course began with an optional "assessment challenge." If students passed with a score of 81 percent or better, they could proceed directly to the unit evaluation. Those who did not take the challenge or who failed it had access to subsequent labs, assignments, and module assessments to prepare for the unit evaluation. Students must receive a score of at least 81 percent to pass the course. Students are allowed three attempts for each unit evaluation.

Kentucky Community and Technical College System

Jay K. Box, president, led the competency-based education programs at the Kentucky Community and Technical College System (KCTCS) while serving as the KCTCS Chancellor from 2009 to 2014. KCTCS is composed of sixteen colleges and more than seventy locations across the Commonwealth of Kentucky. Learn on Demand (LoD) is the KCTCS online, competency-based education degree option that offers online courses in smaller, bite-sized classes. Bite-sized classes are about three to five weeks long and are called "modules."

The modules build toward complete full courses. Students may choose to enroll in LoD: full-course offerings that are fifteen weeks long and include all required modules. LoD students can earn a transferable associate of arts or science degree or more focused degrees in business administration, computer and information technologies, or integrated engineering technology. A Nurse Aide Certificate is also available.[23]

Program Design

As a community college system, general education for transfer and technical programs are the essence of the curriculum. Starting in 2010, statewide committees and councils engaged in an exhaustive general education revision in the KCTCS. This statewide work resulted in an official statewide general education core based on AAC&U's Liberal Education and America's Promise (LEAP) and the Degree Qualifications Profile implemented in the fall of 2012. Additionally, technical education programs in the KCTCS must adhere to the general education components that are aligned with the Secretary's Commission on Achieving Necessary Skills (SCANS). The SCANS report identified three foundational skills and five competencies necessary for success in the workplace.

Based on these frameworks, course materials were developed by subject matter project team leaders for each discipline. Faculty defined the degree, course, and module competencies. Course content, topics, objectives, and competencies were proposed by multi-college discipline collaborations and include open-source and purchased content. Instructional content for practice and review are offered for each lesson, such as practice quizzes, review games, flash cards, interactive presentations, videos, and podcasts. Courses are then reviewed and recommendations made by system-wide curriculum and rules committees, and through the KCTCS faculty senate.

Through the Learn on Demand program, KCTCS colleges bid to develop specific courses, and the successful applicant is provided with instructional design and technology support. Once the course is completed, it undergoes an intensive quality review by instructional designers and discipline faculty serving as subject matter experts. Assessments for each aspect of the course, including competencies, are reviewed and approved by discipline faculty during the same recommendation and quality assurance processes.

Assessment

Assessments take a variety of forms, and mastery is demonstrated through evaluation of assignments in each course content module. All modules begin with a non-graded pre-assessment to provide students with information about existing knowledge and content to focus on each module. Lessons may also include short pre-assessments to further prescribe individual student learning paths. As an example, English composition courses task students with completing a series of essays as part of a portfolio. Each course module provides a variety of checkpoints to outline the essay, submit drafts, and receive feedback prior to submitting their final piece for assessment. Students can add these assignments to build portfolios.

Communication courses follow a similar route. Students are first tasked with completing an outline, then recording two to three minutes of a speech and receiving feedback. In the final assessment, students submit a ten-minute recorded speech with ten visible audience members.

Rubrics are used to assess portfolio components. Other courses may use a series of exams or an end-of-module exam consisting of a variety of question formats. Courses that employ these assessments routinely use authentic assessments as graded assignments.

Authentic assessments reflect knowledge, skills, and abilities that resemble tasks that are used in the real world or in actual situations in which skills will be used. For example, accounting courses task students with creating an accounting plan for a simulated business, and history courses include a series on analyzing primary sources.

Courses may also employ a lab or field activity driven by the competencies. Nursing courses may include a skills task in a clinical setting along with a knowledge-based exam. Industrial engineering courses include labs with mechanical simulators.

In summary, KCTCS built a competency-based education program to ensure student success through their "bite-sized" module approach. These stackable modules led to full courses and ultimately associate degrees that could be transferred to baccalaureate programs or led to degrees in targeted areas in the workforce (e.g., computer and information technologies, business administration, and integrated engineering technology). KCTCS continues to lead the charge in competency-based education for community colleges by providing affordable, relevant, and quality degrees.

Texas Affordable Baccalaureate Program

Van L. Davis, director of innovations in higher education for the Texas Higher Education Coordinating Board, described the Texas Affordable Baccalaureate Program as a partnership forged between the Texas Higher Education Coordinating Board, South Texas College, and Texas A&M University-Commerce, offering a competency-based bachelor of applied sciences in organizational leadership. The degree program is available fully online at Texas A&M-Commerce and as a hybrid at South Texas College.[24]

Program Design

The competency-based bachelor of applied science (BAS) program in organizational leadership focuses on mastery and demonstration of competencies, allows students to earn credit for work and/or military experience, and trains them to apply academic knowledge to global work environments.

The foundation of the degree is the twenty-first-century skills outlined by the American Association of Colleges and Universities (AAC&U), including Knowledge of Human Cultures and the Physical and Natural World, Intellectual and Practical Skills, Personal and Social

Responsibility, and Integrative and Applied Learning. These mastery areas are integrated into the degree program's three component parts: the general education core curriculum, lower-division electives, and upper-division applied coursework.

Upper-division coursework that focuses on degree-specific management skills, such as organizational planning, dynamics of leadership, finance, team building, conflict resolution, and communication, is offered both online and in a traditional face-to-face environment. The program culminates with an applied, digital capstone experience evaluated by faculty and business leaders using a program-specific rubric.

This program is an unprecedented collaboration between a public regional university and a public community college, combining a self-paced, competency-based general education and lower-division elective curriculum with an accelerated cohort-based upper division curriculum. This blend of competencies and accelerated coursework provides students with the leadership skills and knowledge that employers in business, government, and nonprofit settings are seeking.

The degree's first ninety semester credit hours at both institutions are available through shared, self-paced online modules while the remaining thirty upper-division credit hours in the major are available through cohort-based online instruction from Texas A&M University-Commerce or hybrid instruction from South Texas College.

Faculty-driven collaborations are at the heart of the program's development. In 2012–2013, general education faculty members from both schools worked to develop the lower-division competencies, learning outcomes, and enabling objectives. After establishing their disciplinary competencies, these same faculty members reviewed and approved all iterations of the general education competency modules (from early drafts of design documents through the actual modules) and provided detailed instructions and feedback to Pearson, the private partner contracted to develop lower-division competency modules.

For upper-division competencies, faculty from both institutions were joined by K-12 education representatives and area business leaders to create a curriculum that combines twenty-first-century skills, such as leadership and team building, with knowledge in organizational behavior and change, marketing, and management theory.

In an effort to make sure that the program was sufficiently aligned with workforce needs, a variation of the Tuning process was utilized to develop lower-division and upper-division curriculum. AAC&U's LEAP essential learning outcomes were also used to assist in development of the general education competencies.

Students work through a series of competency modules that include a variety of prescriptive and non-prescriptive sources and exercises. These modules include e-texts and other digital media assets as well as discussion boards for collaboration, presentations, videos, and primary documents. Tutorial assistance is available to students on an as-needed basis.

Assessment

Lower-division competencies are assessed at both the beginning and the end of each competency module. Competency assessments vary according to the academic discipline but may include essays, videotaped presentations, artwork, short answers, and research problems. These assessments were developed as part of a partnership between the faculty and Pearson. At the upper division, students complete a portfolio that is evaluated as a part of their capstone experience. This portfolio includes a number of documents, including marketing projects, statistical analysis, essays, and scenario-based case studies. The final portfolio is assessed by a team of experts who carefully review it based upon homegrown rubrics.

Summary of the Case Studies

The three case studies represent a multitude of approaches for building a competency-based education program at community colleges. Broward College, through support from the Department of Labor TA-ACCCT program, developed one associate degree and two certificate (online and hybrid) programs in targeted areas in computer sciences and technology fields.

The Kentucky Community and Technical College System created a series of variable online modules that stack into complete courses for associate degrees, certificates, and diplomas in business, technology, and nursing.

A partnership approach was taken between the Texas Higher Education Coordinating Board, South Texas College, and Texas A&M

University-Commerce, offering a competency-based education bachelor of applied sciences in organizational leadership.

These case studies clearly illustrate successful approaches to building competency-based education programs through grant opportunities, through partnerships, and primarily through faculty-driven aspirations to create new tech-savvy, student-centered pathways to higher education. Community colleges should follow the approach that best meets their institutional and student needs, combine the various approaches, or create a new approach to building competency-based education programs.

DEVELOPING A COMPETENCY-BASED EDUCATION PROGRAM

Key principles and careful planning will facilitate the development of a successful competency-based education program. The following suggestions and questions to consider are a result of the compilation of lessons learned from colleges that are successfully implementing competency-based programs.[25] They also draw upon significant articles outlining observations and steps for planning a competency-based education program.[26]

Should We Develop a Program?

Developing a competency-based education program is time-consuming and requires resources both in people and in funds. Competency-based education has national attention and can result in affordable, accessible, and quality programs, but a college must carefully weigh all aspects and available data to make an informed decision. Following are some specific elements to consider in deciding to move to a competency-based education approach for a program or institution.

Market Research

Does market research support building a competency-based education program? What program(s) and/or credential(s) are supported by market research? What competency-based programs are competitors currently offering? Does the college's advisory board support the potential value of a competency-based education program (e.g., in targeted areas such as business, nursing, technology)? Is there a workforce need for the competency-based education program?

Strategic Direction and University Support

Does a competency-based education program initiative align with the college mission and strategic plan? What is the current college culture in regard to new initiatives, assessment foundation and practices, and use of technology? Does college leadership (e.g., board, president, senior staff, faculty) support the creation of a competency-based education program?

Business Model

Is there funding budgeted for a competency-based education program? What is the business model for the competency-based education program (e.g., tuition, financial aid availability, targeted enrollment goals, faculty model, advisers model)?

Whom to Involve

Competency-based education program development affects all aspects of a college, and it is essential that key roles are represented from the very beginning of the program. Colleges that have already traveled this road suggest that many campus offices be represented through engaging faculty and staff. This can be accomplished through initial large meetings but soon should be divided into working groups.

Institutions should consider the following offices/staff as key stakeholders in moving toward competency: (1) college leadership (e.g., board, president, deans); (2) faculty; (3) information technology; (4) instructional designers; (5) business office; (6) financial aid; (7) admissions; (8) registrar; (9) assessment office and/or psychometrician; (10) advisers; and (11) marketing.

This list of participants may vary according to the college's approach to building a competency-based education program. A key working group in many institutions is the Business Processes Team, which may also include representatives from university-wide data systems, vendors, project management leads, and consultants. Colleges and universities universally recommend that academic and business process personnel work simultaneously with faculty in developing a competency-based education program. A key strategy for building a competency-based program is effective communication among all university offices to share milestones, render critical decisions, and make adjustments to the project plan.

Principles to Consider

When creating competency statements and subsequent learning objectives, it is important to develop robust, valid, and measureable competencies. The competencies are the framework for the curriculum and the assessment and writing effective competencies cannot be understated. Areas to consider when writing competencies are:

1. Is the competency statement measureable, observable, assessable, and actionable?
2. Does the competency reflect the appropriate level of learning (e.g., Bloom's Taxonomy)?
3. Does the competency align with industry or professional standards?
4. How will we know if a student has mastered this competency?
5. What is the credit equivalency of this competency (normally required by regional accreditors and the Department of Education for transferability)?
6. Is there a sequence to the competencies to ensure student success?
7. Are there gaps in the program/credential that are not represented in the competencies (e.g., industry or professional standards, program outcomes in traditional programs, general education requirements)?
8. Did advisory boards, faculty, employers and others provide feedback on the competency statements?
9. Are the competency statements clearly written?[27]

Critical Elements and Questions

The program design in competency-based education programs varies across institutions. Colleges need to consider their institutional culture as well as the needs of the students. It is important to decide the educational pathway for students in the very beginning of the development process. Here are some areas to consider and underlying questions:

Technology

Will the program be fully online, hybrid, or face-to-face? If online, will tools such as adaptive learning, game-based learning, and simulation be used? Will there be a student dashboard to track student progress?

Student Support

How will students be supported? Will there be faculty available for subject matter and content support? Will there be advisers/coaches for student support in areas of engagement, academic policy, and navigation through the competency-based program? What is the schedule for student support (e.g., nights and weekends)? Does the regional accreditor or Department of Education regulate student support (e.g., faculty role)?

Learning Resources

Will the learning resources be primarily textbooks? Will the textbooks be digital and/or paper-based? Will there be open-source materials? Will there be faculty-developed content? Who is responsible for keeping the content up-to-date? Is the content available 24/7? Do students need to engage with the learning materials prior to taking assessments? Who approves the curriculum? How will the curriculum be updated and reflect currency, and how will this be documented and implemented?

Developing and Implementing Assessments

Assessment strategies in building tools and determining how a student will demonstrate mastery of a competency is the heart of a competency-based education program. CBE programs focus on evidence of student learning through rigorous and valid assessments. As the case studies demonstrated, assessment tools vary widely from standardized examinations to faculty developed rubrics. Here are some considerations for assessment development and implementation:

1. Will a variety of assessment strategies be used (e.g., objective-format, performance-based)?
2. Who will develop the assessment tools?
3. How will reliability and validity of assessment tools be determined?
4. Will standardized examinations be used?

5. Who has oversight of the assessment process (e.g., psychometrician, director of CBE assessment)?
6. What assessment policies and procedures need to be developed (e.g., number of times student can take exam)?
7. If using online assessment tools, how will student authentication be determined?
8. What is the approval process for assessments?
9. Will there be signature assignments required for performance-based assessments?
10. Who will grade the performance-based assessments?
11. Will students receive feedback on their performance? If so, how will this be conducted?
12. What is the pass rate for the assessments?[28]

CONCLUSION

Community colleges are well poised to develop competency-based education programs. The new model of competency-based education is an innovative and quality option for delivering higher education credentials, providing an affordable and accessible option for all students while addressing workforce needs. Looking back at the rich history of competency-based education, exploring components of competency-based education, reviewing illustrative case studies, and planning considerations helps set the context for community colleges to continue their good work and spark colleagues to join efforts in creating innovation and excellence in learning.

NOTES

1. White House, *The President's Plan for a Strong Middle Class and a Strong America*, October 5, 2014, http://www.whitehouse.gov/sites/default/files/uploads/sotu_2013_blueprint_embargo.pdf.
2. Anthony P. Carnevale, *21st Century Competencies for College and Career Readiness* (Washington, D.C.: The Georgetown University Center on Education and the Workforce, 2013), 5–9.

3. Martin Van Der Werf and Grant Sabatier, *College of 2020: Students* (Chronicle Research Services: 2009), 1–58.

4. I. Elaine Allen and Jeff Seaman, *Grade Change: Tracking Online Education in the United States* (Babson Survey Research Group & Quahog Research Group, LLC: 2014), 1–45.

5. Amy Laitinen, *Cracking the Credit Hour* (New America Foundation: 2012), 1–24.

6. Hart Research Associates, *It Takes More Than a Major: Employer Priorities for College Learning and Student Success* (April 10, 2013): 1–14.

7. New America Foundation Postsecondary National Policy Institute, *Prior Learning and Competency-Based Education* (New America Foundation: 2013), 1–16.

8. Code of Federal Regulations, Direct Assessment Programs, Title 34, Sec. 668.10.

9. Amy Laitinen, *Cracking the Credit Hour* (New America Foundation: 2012), 1–24.

10. EDUCAUSE Competency-Based Education Webpage, accessed October 5, 2014, http://www.educause.edu/library/competency-based-education-cbe.

11. Council for Adult and Experiential Learning (CAEL) Website, accessed October 5, 2014, http://www.cael.org/what-we-do/competency-based-education http://www.cael.org/what-we-do/competency-based-education.

12. Competency-Based Education Network (C-BEN) Website, accessed October 5, 2014, http://cbe.rfbeta.com/competency-based-education/.

13. American Council on Education and Blackboard, *Clarifying Competency Based Terms* (August 2014): 1–20.

14. Cliff Adelman, Peter Ewell, Paul Gaston, and Carol Geary Schneider, *The Degree Qualifications Profile: A Learning-centered Framework for What College Graduates Should Know and Be Able to Do to Earn the Associate, Bachelor's or Master's Degree* (Lumina Foundation and NILOA: October 2014), 1–55.

15. Cliff Adelman, Peter Ewell, Paul Gaston, and Carol Geary Schneider, *The Degree Qualifications Profile: A Learning-centered Framework for What College Graduates Should Know and Be Able to Do to Earn the Associate, Bachelor's or Master's Degree* (Lumina Foundation and NILOA: January 2014), 1–55.

16. House of Representatives Bill, *Advancing Competency-Based Education Demonstration Project Act of 2014* (2014): 1–16.

17. Patricia A. Book, *All Hands on Deck: Ten Lessons from Early Adopters of Competency-Based Education* (WCET Western Interstate Commission for Higher Education: May 2014), 1–15.

18. AAC&U Liberal Education and America's Promise (LEAP) Essential Learning Outcomes (2008), accessed October 5, 2014, https://www.aacu.org/leap/essential-learning-outcomes.

19. AAC&U Valid Assessment of Learning in Undergraduate Education VALUE Rubrics (2010), accessed October 5, 2014, https://www.aacu.org/value/rubrics.

20. Cliff Adelman, Peter Ewell, Paul Gaston, and Carol Geary Schneider, *The Degree Qualifications Profile: A Learning-centered Framework for What College Graduates Should Know and Be Able to Do to Earn the Associate, Bachelor's or Master's Degree* (Lumina Foundation and NILOA: October 2014), 1–55.

21. U.S. Department of Labor/Employment and Training Administration's Occupational Information Network (O°NET) (2014), accessed October 5, 2014, http://www.onetcenter.org/.

22. "Broward College Accelerated IT Programs," last modified October 25, 2014, http://www.broward.edu/academics/programs/computer/accelerated-computersystemsspecialist/Pages/default.aspx.

23. "KCTCS Learn on Demand," last modified October 25, 2014, http://learnondemand.kctcs.edu/.

24. "Salt Lake Community College School of Applied Technology Electronics Technology," last modified October 25, 2014, http://www.slcc.edu/electronics/.

25. Federal Register, Rules and Regulations, Part II Department of Education, Vol. 75, No. 29, October 29, 2010.

26. "Texas Affordable Baccalaureate Program," last modified October 25, 2014, https://net.educause.edu/ir/library/pdf/NG1229.pdf.

27. Sally M. Johnston and Louis Soares, "Principles for Developing Competency-Based Education Programs," *Change—The Magazine of Higher Learning* (March–April 2014): 1–7.

28. Michael Ray and Lauren Edmonds, *Implementing Competency-Based Education Models: Reducing Classroom Time and Increasing Graduation and Retention Rates* (Education Advisory Board Academic Affairs Forum: 2013), 1–16.

4

INTEGRATED OUTCOMES ASSESSMENT

Nassim Ebrahimi

Community colleges are well positioned to respond to the increased demands for accountability (chapter 2) and the ongoing shifts toward competency-based education (chapter 3). Effective outcomes assessment models embed assessment into existing processes and structures throughout all areas and levels of the institution. They also are best sustained through an institutional culture of assessment that engages all faculty, staff, and students, provides multiple ways of communicating with an emphasis on transparency, and uses meaningful and actionable assessment tools and processes to make it easier to use the results.

This chapter focuses on the current assessment landscape, highlighting the increasing need for well-organized, college-wide assessment systems. A simple framework, a flowchart, is suggested as a means to engage in meaningful dialogue around the development of an effective, efficient, and sustainable assessment system, to foster improvements in learning, and to strengthen the assessment culture. Practical tips, strategies, and examples to create and improve the system are also shared.

THE ASSESSMENT LANDSCAPE

Historically, the emphasis for community colleges has been on ensuring that quality education is accessible to all as institutions responded to the needs of the communities they served. The American Association of Community Colleges captures the community college's role in higher education as being "inclusive institutions that welcome all who desire to learn, regardless of wealth, heritage, or previous academic experience."[1]

Today, community colleges across the nation continue to do a good job of providing access. But they also are placing greater emphasis on success, meeting students where they are, and helping them to achieve their educational goals. The flexibility of community colleges to respond to the multitude of needs of the learners who walk through their doors is unparalleled and is instrumental to their success.

With the shift toward success comes change in the way the nation thinks about the effectiveness of community colleges. Local and national conversations around completion and assessment of student learning, albeit not new to the higher education landscape, increasingly highlight the greater demand for quality assurance and accountability. Not only are community colleges now measured by how many students and what types of students they serve (age, race, gender, previous educational history, etc.), but also by whether students are attaining their educational goals, namely certifications, two-year degrees, or transfer to four-year institutions.

Specifically, the national dialogue around completion, reauthorization of the Higher Education Act, movement toward performance-based funding, utility of regional accreditation, and an increased focus on competency-based education has necessitated transparency and systematic assessment of student learning.

In February 2009, President Obama set a goal for all Americans, declaring by 2020 that America would once again have the highest proportion of college graduates in the world.[2] As one can imagine, the call to increase the number of degree completions has the potential to impact educational quality. However, for colleges that are committed to maintaining their high standards of student learning, the challenge lies in responding to the external pressures to capture data, to quantify success, and to be compared to other colleges relative to their effectiveness in delivering learning outcomes.

Foundations and institutions across the nation have called for similar action and metrics. Lumina Foundation believes that for the nation to remain globally competitive, the "U.S. must increase the proportion of Americans with *high-quality* degrees, certificates and other postsecondary credentials to 60 percent by the year 2025."[3] Harper College outlined plans to "support 10,604 additional degree/certificate completers by 2020."[4] And, as recently as August 2014, the California Community College System—the nation's largest—announced a plan to "increase the number of students earning certificates, degrees or transferring to four-year institutions by nearly a quarter of a million over the next 10 incoming freshman classes."[5]

Others have pooled resources and expertise across the country together to move the needle on student success and decrease the equity gap. For example, Achieving the Dream, Inc., values "evidence-based, student centered . . . continuous improvement [to help] low-income students and students of color complete their education and obtain market-valued credentials."[6]

The emphasis on completion, however, is occurring at a time when lawmakers are looking for ways to hold colleges accountable for their costs and outcomes. Many believe the reauthorization of the Higher Education Act is an opportunity for the government to pursue changes to the accreditation system and increase the focus on less expensive models of learning (e.g., competency-based education).

Additionally, with national financial pressures, federal support of student learning through Pell Grants also is under scrutiny. Regional accreditors have responded to these pressures by increasing the rigor and demand of systematic assessment of student outcomes and subsequent improvements. For example, the Middle States Commission on Higher Education has revised their standards to "embed assessment in each of the areas reflective of the need to increase accountability and transparency."[7]

With a renewed spotlight on the reauthorization of the Higher Education Act, developments in competency-based education and the streamlining of degree pathways have also gained momentum. Colleges are revising their curricula through the lens of core competencies (e.g., common skill sets such as communication and critical thinking), and the alignment of course- and program-level outcomes as opposed to solely the sequencing of courses, necessitating a renewed focus on the systematic measurement of outcomes at the course, program, and institution levels. Degree pathways and curriculum maps, albeit not new to higher education, are gaining renewed attention as tools to ensure efficient and quality learning opportunities for students.

Likewise, as funding at the local and national levels has decreased, the federal government and some states have increasingly moved toward performance-based funding models. As of September 2013, a total of thirty-nine states had adopted, or are engaged in formal discussions that could lead to, performance-based funding (e.g., Pennsylvania, Virginia, Texas, and Tennessee).[8] At the state level, funding formulas generally rely on metrics such as general and subgroup student outcome indicators (e.g., graduation rates, number of degrees/certificates awarded per FTE, job placement rates, success on licensing exams, etc.), progress outcome indicators (e.g., developmental course completion, number of students transferring to four-year institutions, etc.), and/or high-need subject outcome indicators (e.g., STEM fields, nursing, etc.).

Nationally, however, existing accountability measures in higher education do not adequately and appropriately measure the unique mission of community colleges. For example, the College Scorecard compares institutions on fall enrollment, graduation rates of first-time full-time students, loan default rate, and median borrowing.[9]

For many higher education institutions, these metrics—graduation rates, for example—may be a reflection of the population they serve, and not the quality of the educational services. Traditionally defined graduation rates are often an inaccurate picture of a community college's efficacy because first-time full-time students are only a small percentage of those served by community colleges, and these measures exclude returning students and part-time students.

The mobility of students across institutions is also not considered. Today's learners are "increasingly attending multiple institutions across a region or nationally before completing their degree."[10] Yet the typical method for calculating graduation rates, as stipulated by federal legislation and captured in the College Scorecard, counts only those students who enroll full-time and then start and finish at their first college or university. Several promising efforts in recent years have attempted to address this problem.

The Student Achievement Measure (SAM) initiative attempts to better account for the success of these students by not only including full- and part-time students in the cohort, but those who are attending the institution for the first time (including transfer students).[11] SAM also tracks students' movements across institutions, enabling a more accurate picture of progress and completion. Equally important, SAM also aligns to metrics put forward by the Voluntary Framework of Accountability (VFA).

In 2012, the American Association for Community Colleges, in partnership with the Association of Community College Trustees and the College Board, finalized the metrics of the VFA to more accurately capture the mission of the institutions they serve. The VFA tracks the progress and completion of a wide range of community college students, including those progressing through developmental education, career and workforce development, adult basic education, and their respective student learning outcomes. For example, the VFA "uses a retrospective cohort tracking method for measuring the progress (after 2 years) and outcomes (after 6 years) of a student population that includes all students who enter in the fall who are first-timers at that college and attend part time or full time."[12]

To date, over one hundred institutions have voluntarily joined the VFA and are benefiting from the comparative benchmarking data to which they have access. Of the VFA metrics, however, the student learning outcomes component is yet to be defined, but the importance of systematically measuring and sharing outcomes assessment data is underscored by encouragement to use the Transparency Framework developed by the National Institute for Learning Outcomes Assessment (NILOA) in the VFA process.

Similarly, created in 2011, the Transparency Framework is meant to assist institutions in guiding and evaluating the extent to which evidence of student learning outcomes assessment and its results are readily accessible to various audiences. The framework guides the components and communication important to the increased need for accountability and transparency. The components of the Transparency Framework include: clearly articulated student learning outcomes statements; assessment plans; assessment resources to assist faculty and staff; current assessment activities; evidence of student learning; and use of assessment results for improvement, institutional decision-making, problem identification, planning, goal setting, faculty development, course revision, program review, and accountability or accreditation self-study.[13]

The Framework does not, however, guide what learning to assess or how to assess it. Instead, it only offers a guide to communicating existing institutional practices. The institutional assessment practices themselves—their quality, efficiency, and sustainability—are at the heart of an assessment culture built around an assessment system.

Colleges Respond

To respond to this changing landscape and increased accountability demands, colleges across the nation may have been too quick to put assessment processes and procedures in place. These hastily developed processes include course, program, unit, and institutional-level assessments involving all areas of the college: instructional and non-instructional. This often piecemeal approach to assessment has, in many cases, led to disjointed processes that are redundant and may not be used to their fullest potential in informing other student learning assessment processes and improvements.

For example, initially course-level assessment practices received a lot of attention and colleges were quick to emphasize systematic assessment of every course. As program outcomes and general education competencies are now becoming the focus, separate processes are being instituted to address this new need instead of maximizing the use of information that has already been collected at the course level to inform programmatic and institution-level learning outcomes assessment reporting.

The components of a college's assessment system are often like pieces of a puzzle that are not yet put together. Each is identifiable and useful on its own but is removed from the context of the system as a whole. Consequently, when assembled together, the daunting number of assessment processes often produces a larger, albeit blurry picture for the viewer, much like the purchasing and use of technology in higher education. Software is purchased to meet individual needs of areas (e.g., assessment, advising, online learning, early alert, predictive analytics, etc.), addressing the immediate demand.

However, colleges now face the dilemma of having many different technological solutions that do not interface with one another and often require the maintenance of redundant information in separate systems. The emphasis now, similar to that in assessment, is on finding ways to integrate technologies or introduce tools that allow seamless communication among systems.

With these increasing external demands, over time, internal tensions have also grown as colleges attempt to respond by creating additional pieces to their assessment practices or to retrofit old pieces into larger, mismatched systems.

Ewell, in his occasional paper for the National Institute for Learning Outcomes Assessment, reflects on the tensions often felt by institutions around outcomes assessment that may affect an assessment system's efficacy, efficiency, and sustainability. Some faculty and staff view assessment as added work only being done to satisfy accountability pressures with no long-term benefit for them or their students. Many are looking for the magic bullet that will satisfy all demands on them so that they can focus on their classrooms.[14]

These views, however, jeopardize the fundamental purpose of assessment as part of ongoing, reflective improvements to student learning—indeed, a focus on their classroom. But if assessment is truly embedded into the fabric of an institution, is used at all levels to improve the student learning experience, and is designed with efficiency and sustainability in mind, these tensions can be alleviated, giving way to meaningful assessment practices that improve student learning.

To achieve this, many institutions look to borrow pieces or whole models from other institutions—a one-size-fits-all approach. Often this only adds to the tensions and is perceived as an imposed model as opposed to one that accounts for the unique nature of the institution, owned by the institution's faculty and staff.

A better approach instead is to build a customized system that involves all areas of the college and can respond to current and future demands while allowing for continuous improvement to the assessment system and student learning. A customized model must account for the institution's unique mission, vision, values, goals, strategic plan, size, programs, student body, faculty and staff expertise, available technological and financial resources and priorities, and organizational structure and culture.

Across all community colleges, no matter their variations in mission, size, resources, etc., their underlying purpose is the same: student learning. The emphasis on learning must reside at the root of all assessment systems, grounding and aligning all assessments and the resulting improvements. Learning should remain at the forefront of every conversation and decision, and should serve as the common thread across institutional assessment systems.

It is now *imperative* that the pieces of the assessment puzzle be put together. The changing landscape demands and requires system-level thinking of assessment to coordinate and integrate efforts to move student learning forward and improve college processes. In particular, systematic and efficient systems and processes that reduce redundancies and maximize the use of data and information can greatly alleviate internal tensions around assessment.

Often, faculty and staff question the efficacy of assessment processes and reporting, fearing that their hard work and efforts will result in a report that sits on the shelf. If processes are built to inform other, related processes and are aligned, as information is collected at one level (e.g., course-level assessment), the information can systematically inform other efforts at that level (e.g., other course-level assessment projects) and those at higher levels (e.g., program, unit, or institution levels).

Additionally, if assessment data is valued at all levels of the institution (faculty, department chairs/directors, deans, vice presidents, presidents, board of trustees) not only to meet the external reporting demands, but also to inform key decisions at the college, faculty and staff engaging in learning outcomes assessment will see the value of their efforts and will be more motivated to contribute in the future. This, in turn, contributes to sustaining assessment systems by affirming that the assessment of what a student knows and is able to do is a fundamental part of ongoing, reflective improvements in student learning.

So how does an institution build such a system? How can an existing system be improved? How can it then be shared to begin the process of moving an institution to embracing assessment as a fundamental component of the educational process? The next section walks through the process of self-evaluation and systems-thinking necessary to begin reframing the college-wide assessment dialogue.

Where Things Stand Now

In July 2011, at the Best Practices in Institutional Effectiveness conference, Dr. Barbara Walvoord shared an assessment system tool to view, evaluate, and communicate college-wide assessment processes.[15] This simple framework, a flowchart, has the potential to greatly change the way institutions communicate and systematically evaluate assessment processes. In this section, the focus is on how to create the system flowchart, and in subsequent sections, how to use the tool to improve processes, and increase buy-in among faculty, staff, and students.

As assessment processes are being reviewed and efficiencies are being created to increase sustainability and efficacy, foundational assumptions must also be preserved. The key assumptions should be:

- *Assessments must ultimately inform improvements in teaching and learning.* Assessment for the sake of assessment or only to respond to external demands must be avoided. Instead, meaningful, actionable assessment processes should be emphasized that can not only be used to improve the student learning, but can also inform external stakeholders.
- *Benefits to student learning should outweigh the costs of the assessment process.* The cost-benefit analysis is crucial to determining the design and support of assessment processes. Benefits to the students, learning environment, and institution need to outweigh costs, such as time, technological support, faculty and staff resources, etc. This is probably the most challenging key assumption to preserve. Many institutions react to regional or federal accountability pressures by purchasing technological solutions, for example, without first fully integrating the tool's capabilities into the assessment system, or taking the time and effort needed to maximize its use across the college. These knee-jerk reactions to external pressures can undermine assessment processes and systems. Many successful Fortune 500 companies have benefited

from decision support systems and analytics platforms that enable data-supported decisions from the CEO to the line manager. In the next decade, innovative community colleges should do the same.

• *Assessment processes must comply with accrediting body, state, and federal demands for transparency and accountability.* Assessment processes and systems that embed the use of information already gathered for external reporting enhance their efficiency by reducing redundancies in their efforts.

Of course, there are many ways to communicate assessment processes. Many community colleges now have detailed assessment plans, handbooks, forms, templates, examples, etc., to guide and communicate with all constituencies. These tools and documents, however, do not necessarily provide a simple representation of the assessment system as a whole that could enable faculty, staff, and students to see the importance of their roles and efforts, and enable senior administration to see the value of outcomes assessment in daily decision-making. A simple visual representation may be the solution (see Figure 4.1).

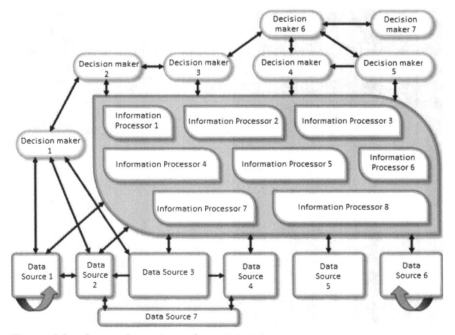

Figure 4.1.   A sample system of assessment.

A critical look at the current state of affairs allows the review and communication of existing processes to support assessment. The process of creating and the subsequent reviewing of the assessment system flowchart allows for the review of critical questions: Are appropriate faculty/staff supports in place to sustain assessment efforts? Are the results used to facilitate improvements? If not, is the data relevant or is it shared in a way that is conducive to its use? How are results reported and/or shared with the college community?

The initial creation of the flowchart representing the assessment processes and system should involve a representative cross-section of those most involved in data collection, processing, and decision-making. Leaders, representatives from key committees and offices, and faculty and staff from instructional and non-instructional areas of the college can provide the varied perspectives needed to accurately capture current processes. The brainstorming activity that follows, identifying the pieces of the puzzle, not only helps to inform the creation of the visual representation, but begins the open, critical dialogue that can strengthen the overall assessment culture.

To begin, existing data collection processes and sources (see Figure 4.1) need to be identified. Examples include:

- college-wide surveys (e.g., Community College Survey of Student Engagement, Survey of Entering Student Engagement, Faculty Survey of Student Engagement, Noel-Levitz, Personal Assessment of the College Environment);
- data reporting to external stakeholders (state and federal metrics);
- systematic assessment of college-wide competencies, general education, programs, and/or courses;
- curriculum map;
- assessment of non-instructional units; and/or
- key institutional performance indicators.

The next list should be of the processors of information: those who design, implement, analyze, and/or disseminate the results of the data collection processes (see Figure 4.1). These processors can range from particular departments or positions within the organization, such as Institutional Research and/or Learning Outcomes Assessment offices, to committees within the shared governance structure, and/or additional committees or groups that may support assessment processes.

The final listing is that of the decision-makers, those who truly review the information and use it to make curricular, policy, fiduciary, and other critical decisions at the college (see Figure 4.1). These three key categories (data collection processes and sources, processors of information, and decision-makers) are the foundation of the graphical representation of the system, though there is no ideal number of each.

How the pieces work together is the heart of the system. Putting the pieces of the puzzle together, capturing the relationships between the data sources, processors of information, and decision-makers is the key to understanding how the parts of the system work and inform one another. The direction and strength of the relationships, depicted by single- or double-headed arrows, represent the flow of information both forward toward decision-making, and feedback to process improvement. Both are important and necessary for ensuring a strong system that is well positioned to respond to changing demands. Not captured through the arrows, but important to consider as the flowchart is being created, are the communication mechanisms in place to share results and improvements (e.g., newsletters, emails, presentations, professional development workshops, formal reports, etc.).

Often, during the creation of the graphical representation of the system, specific processes and procedures come under review. It is important during this part of the process, the initial creation of the graphical representation, to capture the current processes at the institution without making any changes or decisions about improvements until the complete system is documented. This preserves the essence of the purpose of the flowchart—to facilitate more coordinated dialogue for thoughtful systematic improvements, not just adjustments to individual processes devoid of considering their impact on the system.

Where Do We Go from Here?

Putting the puzzle together is just the start. Once the initial assessment system flowchart is created, the meaningful work of assessing the assessment processes at the college begins. The flowchart is a valuable tool in representing the systems components and relationships within the system to guide dialogue around:

- What is working well?
- What can be removed or enveloped in other processes?
- Is the system working efficiently?
- Is the system sustainable? Are appropriate resources in place to support the system, including roles and responsibilities of committees and assessment offices?
- Are there redundancies?
- Are the existing data being used to inform other processes in addition to improvements to the learning environment?
- Are the results being communicated and used efficiently and effectively?
- Are the processes, results, and improvements made as a result being communicating effectively?
- Are additional information/assessment processes needed? Are there any gaps? Are there any loops in communication or action that require closing?
- Is the system responsive to all current and future external demands?

The open, honest dialogue about the components of the system and how they work together is critical to effectively improving the system as a whole. The flowchart allows for the identification of needed processes to better address any deficiencies that may exist and to remove redundant processes or parts of processes. The shift toward strategic, meaningful, efficient processes greatly impacts a college's ability to sustain the system and strengthen a culture of assessment.

CASE STUDY: ANNE ARUNDEL COMMUNITY COLLEGE

Anne Arundel Community College (AACC), in Arnold, Maryland, serves over fifty-three thousand students a year. There are over 850 full-time faculty and staff, and the college offers over one hundred associate's degrees and certificates, and over one thousand courses.

In July 2011, the director of Learning Outcomes Assessment (LOA) was hired after the position had been vacant for more than four years. Because the college's self-study for reaccreditation was a little less than three years away, it was critical to determine the scope of assessment work that had continued in the absence of an office to coordinate existing efforts. A review of all current reports and documents began immediately.

All available comprehensive and annual program reviews from the 2008 reaccreditation, noting all referenced assessment processes, were reviewed. Structured meetings with deans and department chairs provided insight into the depth and scope of course-level processes occurring. All college manuals and charters were reviewed with an eye to assessment's contributions to constituency groups and shared governance structures.

As information was received, pieces of AACC's existing assessment puzzle and their relationship to one another became more apparent. Additionally, many individuals offered their personal impressions of the usefulness and impact of the data and processes. These reflections were noted and were used to guide future improvements. By January 2012, AACC's first assessment system flowchart was created. The process of creating the flowchart revealed several immediate improvements that were needed:

- a critical review of the comprehensive and annual program review processes was needed to reduce redundancies and increase its value to improvements in student learning;
- the college-wide core competencies had not been systematically assessed since the position of director of LOA had been vacated;
- a college-wide curriculum map did not exist to guide strategic and efficient assessment; and
- the many assessment processes identified did not have adequate support for an institution of its size.

Given the budgetary limitations for hiring additional full-time staff for the Office of LOA, the Assessment Fellows Program was launched. The Program brought together a cohort of faculty and staff who would receive monthly professional development training to enable their support of assessment processes on the ground.

In the years that followed, the assessment system flowchart became the foundational tool to:

- systematically review assessment processes;
- make improvements to the system with an eye to how the changes may affect other processes; and
- communicate the importance of the assessment work and progress to all levels of the college organizational structure.

Consequently, committees, subcommittees, and fellows more clearly understood their roles in the system and how their work affected assessment and reporting overall. In essence, they all had a much greater understanding of their piece of the puzzle. For the Office of LOA, as the entity of the college that leads, coordinates, and supports all assessments of learning, the system of assessment flowchart not only helps as a communication tool, but is reviewed annually when identifying the current practices and future directions of the college in the LOA Plan.

SUSTAINING THE ASSESSMENT SYSTEM

Of course the assessment system flowchart itself is easy to maintain. However, the content of what it represents must be regularly reviewed and improved as needed. The sustainability of the assessment system of a college relies on the financial resources, and more importantly, the faculty and staff and their involvement, communication streams, and acknowledgment and recognition.

Integrating faculty and staff involvement throughout the fabric of the assessment system is the key to its success. The participation of these individuals is not only critical to data collection efforts, but they are the driving force behind the effective use of the results to improve the learning environment for students. Instructional faculty and staff, both full-time and adjunct, along with non-instructional staff in student services, have the potential to make the greatest impact on the retention and success of students.

Having meaningful, actionable, and timely data can strengthen their efforts. For these integral parts of the system to be fully engaged in assessment processes, the design and implementation of assessment processes should also involve faculty and staff across the college: credit and non-credit, instructional and non-instructional, full-time and contingent.

Ground-up or grassroots efforts have the greatest "buy-in" and are most effective in enacting change where needed. Colleges that rely solely on the work of institutional research or learning outcomes assessment office staff struggle with the use of results and/or implementing changes as a result. Buy-in needs to be a priority from the first conversations around what to assess and how.

How can a community college ensure active involvement of faculty and staff across the college? The answer is simple, at least on paper: build or embed assessment processes into structures within shared governance, or create groups that are processors of information in the assessment system; garner full support from college administration; ensure that every committee/assessment group at the college is representative of all key constituencies; and provide multiple means of communication and recognition.

Shared Governance Structures or Assessment Groups

The organizational and shared governance structures within community colleges are as unique as their missions, sizes, students, communities, etc. Therefore the examples shared here around types of structures are only meant to demonstrate the multitude of ways that colleges can involve faculty and staff in their assessment system, primarily by embedding structures into the fabric of their institution. No one way works across all colleges, and not all should be implemented simultaneously. The existing culture and structures should be carefully reviewed before revising or creating new structures for assessment. Sometimes, the most efficient change is to embed assessment into an existing structure. Following is a list of the types of committees/structures that allow faculty and staff involvement in the assessment system.

- Assessment committees/councils
- General education committees
- Curriculum committees

- Assessment fellows
- Data teams
- Faculty/staff liaisons to their departments
- Departmental assessment committees

The offices and people responsible for leading and guiding assessment processes are the key to ensuring that the system works efficiently and effectively. They must work closely with each committee or group to ensure that their work is not redundant and supports the system as a whole. Entities at the college responsible for providing data must also work closely with the assessment staff to ensure timely and appropriate sharing of results. Additionally, those who analyze the data can inform collection processes by sharing what information is already collected, minimizing redundancies of data collection. First, maximize available information before engaging in new assessment processes.

Garnering Full Support of the College's Leadership

Support from the college leadership is critical for many reasons. They range from the most obvious, resource allocation, to the less obvious, the use of assessment data in decision-making processes. College leadership, in many respects, sets the tone for assessment systems. If they attend events, encourage and recognize faculty and staff, and consider assessment results as they are making programmatic and budgetary decisions, they are modeling the infusion of assessment and data-informed decision-making into the culture of an institution. All stakeholders will take notice. Most importantly, the impact of supportive leadership is felt at all levels of the system. When faculty and staff see that their assessment endeavors are supported, not only through financial means, but that this information is considered in decisions around programmatic and course-level improvement, and when they feel that their work is acknowledged, assessment becomes a priority for faculty and staff.

Some college leaders believe they are supporting assessment processes when they remind a college community that their assessment efforts contribute to external reporting, but this can undermine a system. The focus should remain on student learning and improvements to the learning environment. Reporting and accountability are important, but they should not drive assessment conversations. Conversely, the system needs to be continuously tweaked as needed to make it as useful as possible for decision-making.

Support from the college leadership can be garnered in many ways, including but not limited to:

- routine reports at meetings;
- annual assessment reports;
- integrating assessment into formal budgetary processes by aligning assessment and budgetary cycles;
- involving leadership in review processes;
- inviting participation in data-collection or scoring processes;
- advocating for participation in college-wide professional development;
- sharing national dialogue and assessment opportunities;
- showcasing assessment endeavors; and
- engaging external consultants to help articulate the value of assessment and ease the process.

CONCLUSION

This perfect storm of shifting national trends and demands in higher education necessitates effective, efficient, and sustainable systems of assessment to not only respond to these external demands, but also to maintain the standards of a quality education. A simple system of assessment flowchart, as presented here, can facilitate a critical review of processes and structures, garner college-wide support, and serve as a tool to strategically enhance processes and improvements to student learning. Five key steps can lead to creating the flowchart and assuring effective use:

1. bring together a representative cross-section of those most involved in data collection, processing, and decision-making to identify data-collection processes and sources, processors of information, and key decision-makers;

2. identify how the pieces of the system fit together;

3. take a critical look at how the system is working;

4. make improvements as needed; and

5. use the tool to systematically assess processes and engage faculty and staff across the college in using assessment to improve learning.

Continuously engaging the college community in assessment dialogue and processes is key to the sustainability and continuous improvement of the system, all focused on fostering student success.

NOTES

1. "About Community Colleges," American Association of Community Colleges, accessed October 31, 2014, http://www.aacc.nche.edu/AboutCC/Pages/default.aspx.

2. "Remarks of President Barack Obama—As Prepared for Delivery Address to Joint Session of Congress," last modified February 24, 2009, http://www.whitehouse.gov/the_press_office/Remarks-of-President-Barack-Obama-Address-to-Joint-Session-of-Congress.

3. See http://www.luminafoundation.org/advantage/document/goal_2025/2013-Lumina_Strategic_Plan.pdf.

4. "Completion," last modified July 25, 2014, http://goforward.harpercollege.edu/about/leadership/planning/college_plan/ipac/completion/.

5. "California Community Colleges Sets Goal to Increase Student Completions by Nearly a Quarter of a Million Statewide," last modified August 27, 2014, http://californiacommunitycolleges.cccco.edu/Portals/0/DocDownloads/PressReleases/AUG2014/PR_BOG_GOALS_for_8-27-14_Press_Conf_news_release_FINAL_8-22-14.pdf.

6. "About Us," Achieving the Dream, accessed October 31, 2014, http://achievingthedream.org/about-us.

7. Middle States Commission on Higher Education, *Standards for Accreditation and Requirements for Affiliation* (Philadelphia: Middle States Commission on Higher Education, 2014).

8. Janice Nahra Friedel, Zoë Mercedes Thornton, Mark M. D'Amico, and Stephen G. Katsinas, "Performance-based Funding: The National Landscape," *Education Policy Center* (September 2013).

9. "College Scorecard," College Affordability and Transparency Center, accessed October 31, 2014, http://collegecost.ed.gov/scorecard/index.aspx.

10. "College Students Still on the Move," National Student Clearinghouse, accessed October 31, 2014, http://www.studentclearinghouse.org/about/media_center/press_releases/files/release_2014-05-06.pdf.

11. "About," Student Achievement Measure, accessed October 31, 2014, http://www.studentachievementmeasure.org/about.

12. "Voluntary Framework of Accountability," American Association of Community Colleges, accessed October 31, 2014, http://vfa.aacc.nche.edu/Documents/VFAOutcomesReportWebFINAL.pdf.

13. National Institute for Learning Outcomes Assessment, Transparency Framework. Urbana, IL: University of Illinois and Indiana University, National Institute for Learning Outcomes Assessment (NILOA), 2011. Retrieved from: http://www.learningoutcomesassessment.org/TransparencyFramework.htm.

14. P. T. Ewell, "Assessment, Accountability, and Improvement: Revisiting the Tension" (NILOA Occasional Paper No.1). Urbana, IL: University of Illinois and Indiana University, National Institute for Learning Outcomes Assessment, 2009).

15. Annual Institute on Best Practices in Institutional Effectiveness 2011, Dr. Walvoord materials.

5

ENGAGING FACULTY

Marcus M. Kolb

With a comprehensive assessment plan in place, informed by innovations like competency-based education and a new view of accountability, the most crucial task begins. While administrators may be tempted to take the needed improvements described in these chapters and start to swing a heavy ax, no changes like those described here will be lasting or meaningful if they are not driven by the faculty. The faculty needs to be aggressively engaged by academic leadership to embrace these needed improvements and chart a course forward for the community college.

This chapter rests on one simple assumption: faculty are the essential element of any increase in success and completion for students at any level of higher education. This in no way diminishes key support functions, filled with talented and committed people, but faculty stand alone in one very important way. They are the only truly compulsory element of higher education. A student taking a course must, in some way, interact with the faculty member leading the course, even if it is only to listen. Therefore, any solution designed to improve student success requires that faculty be fully engaged.

This is not to imply that faculty alone are responsible for the current predicament of declining public confidence, stagnant completion, apparent skill gaps in graduates, and questionable learning outcomes. Certainly, they are a part of the "problem" as many define it, but they are not solely, or even principally, responsible. Indeed, it has been a proverbial team effort to get to this crucial juncture for many institutions.

Considering all of the good advice and innovations presented in the previous chapters, from designing sound assessment to engaging accreditors, transitioning to competencies to rethinking credentials, faculty are central to their successful implementation. Strategies for bringing faculty to these conversations, then, are crucial if higher education is to be successful in transforming itself. Too often, though, on campuses, those in leadership roles are reluctant to "engage" faculty.

Traditional, monolithic views of faculty hold that they are difficult to deal with, hide behind academic freedom (an often misapplied concept in this setting), take a Darwinist approach to student success, and mostly decline to participate when asked to do more to improve the work of supporting student success and degree completion. Even at the community college, where the composition of the faculty, and the types of students in the seats or on the screen, are often different from those of many four-year colleges and universities, these stereotypes, and some faculty who actually fit the stereotypes, persist.

One critical consequence of this reluctance to engage faculty in institutional transformation is the emergence of alternate strategies for working around faculty instead of with them. Committees are convened to address student learning, assessment of student learning, or a curricular matter like general education, with only token faculty representation. In the cases where faculty cannot be avoided, the same folks are drawn upon, over and over, knowing that they are "safe" to work with.

In fact, one could argue that much of what is done in student services is a "work-around" for roles that faculty can and should be filling. This topic is another book entirely, but the point is that we have generally done a poor job of putting faculty in roles that, in fact, they are best prepared to execute.

What remains is a set of strategies for how to best engage faculty in the work described earlier in this book. There are many ways to think about the challenge of inviting new, enthusiastic voices into the conversation while also finding room for slow adopters or even downright naysayers. All need a place at the table because all bring value to the conversations.

BARRIERS AND OPPORTUNITIES

Faculty Are Not All the Same

Attempting to offer approaches to working with faculty, of course, risks the common mistake of thinking of faculty as a monolith. And higher education personnel have fostered this approach through attributing particular dispositions to the faculty over the decades. For example, faculty are intractable in their teaching and assessment approaches. Or, faculty believe that they are already using good assessment techniques. Or, faculty see their role as teachers, and the responsibility of learning falls on the students.

Staff and leadership have heard many of these things in many settings, and many have probably hidden behind them to stay inactive in propelling meaningful change on campus. Many of these assumptions, and others, are relevant to conversations about teaching, learning, and assessment, but to attribute them to all faculty is to start with a deficit mentality. Engaging faculty should not be an uphill battle, but for leaders to enter a meeting with jaws set, ready to be rebuffed or, worse, driven from the room by pure apathy, is halfway to defeat. A whole set of approaches to draw upon is available, and required, when the time is right.

A talented former colleague once framed it best. When trying to bring anyone into a conversation that they may be reluctant to engage, begin with the following question: What problem does this person have that I can help them solve? When speaking specifically of faculty, there are many problems they describe when asked what most bothers them:

- My students don't seem interested in learning.
- Assessment conversations make me surrender control of my classroom.
- We have done this learning outcomes stuff over and over for several decades now.
- My time is too precious to devote to all of these extraneous activities.
- I know best what students should learn about my discipline—not legislators, not employers, not the general public, not accreditors, and not administrators.

All of the above have some face validity. A lot is asked of faculty. They are under increased scrutiny, which, when responses to the scrutiny are required, can detract from their time with students. And many stakeholders have their hand in the conversation about teaching, learning, and assessment. All of these issues, though, only serve to argue for why faculty should readily engage in these discussions about defining learning and enhancing student success right now.

Clearly defining student learning outcomes and competencies, and creating authentic assessments that are well-aligned with the desired outcomes and competencies, can make these "problems" go away. Clear outcomes allow students to see the relationship between what they are learning in a given course and their chosen occupation or field. Assessment conversations, in fact, empower faculty to define what they are teaching and facilitate measurement and assurance that students are, in fact, learning what they are teaching.

Learning outcomes require constant revision and improvement to keep up with new trends in academic fields and places of work. And time spent on teaching, and the improvement of teaching, should be central to the professional life of any faculty member.

Many of the objections faculty raise can be reduced to a single point of contention: I am losing control of what I do. The work of improving teaching, learning, and assessment, however, provides the ultimate antidote. Even many supportive stakeholders are asking hard questions because they have lost faith in the higher education enterprise.

Where it was once assumed that faculty knew best, now students fail to graduate in an appropriate span of time or in appropriate numbers. Employers tell institutions that graduates are ill-prepared to enter the workforce, and they have been telling us that, referencing the same skills, for years now.[1] With the resources that federal and state governments are pouring into institutions, and with flat or even declining outcomes in terms of graduates to show for it, legislators, too, are involving themselves in more invasive ways.

Losing Control

Faculty are the key to keeping the control they cherish. *Control* is a loaded word in this context. While higher education professionals quickly move from "control" in the context of faculty to misapplied notions of academic freedom and intransigence, we must acknowledge

that faculty are operating in an environment where their sense of owner-
ship of the curriculum, both in content and delivery, is under constant
scrutiny. Consequently, some defensiveness is to be expected, and
accounted for, at the very beginning of embarking on work in student
learning and success.

Faculty have been hearing from many on many fronts about how
higher education is failing students. One of the most notable was the
book *Academically Adrift*.[2] Likewise, accreditor demands for increased
evidence of student learning, sometimes verified by a third party, is an
implicit criticism. Surveys of employers show consistent deficiencies in
key workplace skills. Faculty also have watched as the Common Core
State Standards have been adopted by dozens of states, indicating a federal appetite to dig deeply into curriculum and make demands.[3]

Federal politicos regularly tell the public about the lavish life that
faculty lead.[4] In addition, now states are adopting policies that partially
reward institutions for students who persist and graduate, signifying
even more intervention may be on the way.

In the past, faculty at community colleges were somewhat immune
to these critiques, as they did not represent very sexy targets. However,
now they are more closely aligned with faculty at four-year institutions,
share professional and personal relationships, and interact with each
other in the same disciplinary circles. In short, they, too, can feel the
heat, and it has encouraged them to close ranks and tell the outside
world that things are under control. All the while, they wait anxiously for
someone else to step in and start to make demands. And then those administrators and leaders charged with improving learning outcomes on
campuses arrive at their door, confirming that the threat is everywhere.

So, for all of these reasons, whether real or imagined, it is crucial to
make this work faculty-owned, and not just in a political sense. One way
to better engage faculty, to insulate them from criticism, and to keep
them invested in the process of improving teaching and learning is to
charge them with making change, and then give them the tools to do
the work. That is why the work of Tuning USA is so powerful, and the
outcomes so well-received.[5] Not only does Tuning place the curricular
reins in the hands of faculty, but it also gives them a clear road map to
follow in order to develop sound student learning outcomes that serve
themselves, their students, employers, and the community.

Tuning, adapted to the U.S. context, involves five steps.[6] First, identify a faculty team, representing a given discipline. Second, provide that team with "reference points"—resources that inform what is crucial for a student to know and to be able to do at the completion of a credential. Third, develop a set of student learning outcomes based upon the reference points and informed by the expertise of the faculty team. Fourth, test those proposed outcomes with other faculty, graduates, employers, and current students, checking to see if the proposed outcomes truly represent what is crucial to the discipline. Finally, apply the feedback to improve the outcomes in whatever fashion the faculty see fit. Then the process is repeated regularly to accommodate evolutions in the given field, but the first pass provides the bedrock upon which future work can be more efficiently accomplished.

Faculty seem to prosper with this technique, engaging in deep conversation about learning and assessment, with no worries about losing control of their curriculum. While this approach may not be the best for all—some American faculty are naturally resistant to a process developed in Europe—some version of it is exactly what is required both to accomplish renovation of the curriculum and to allow the renovation to be led by the faculty, maintaining "control," with other stakeholders assured that their interests will be met.

Faculty Identities

Tuning USA also illuminated some other key considerations. In strategizing how to work with faculty, the issue of faculty identity—those whom faculty view themselves as affiliated with—provides insight into effective approaches. At small institutions, the kinds of places where all faculty can meet in a single room, faculty identity may very well be that of the institution. When asked the questions, what do you do, the faculty member may respond, "I teach at X college." However, at institutions that are large, identification with a particular program or discipline may be more common. "I teach biology," or "I am a journalist."

Another possibility is the primary role a faculty member plays off campus. "I am a contractor" or "I am a chemist" might fall from the lips of adjunct faculty who are also holding down full-time jobs in their respective fields. All of these statements provide some clues about how to appeal to faculty and invite them into the conversation on teaching and learning. When arranging faculty into groups to execute assessment design or revisions, or to raise awareness on campus about student learning, similar groupings work best: e.g., biologists with other biologists, instructors from Fictional College with other faculty from Fictional College. This is something of a "unit of analysis" approach to working with faculty. Good strategy begins with understanding the faculty's sense of affiliation and identity.

In the context of Tuning USA, when faculty groups from different institutions first convened, the lines between institutions quickly dissolved as the economists from different institutions quickly realized that their training and orientation was similar, as did the psychologists and sociologists. This orientation to discipline appeared to transcend institutional prestige and type. On the other hand, in working with faculty at many small private colleges on the issue of student learning outcomes in the context of the Degree Qualifications Profile, the affiliation to the institution and its students made liberal arts faculty open to working with engineers in a way that was not evident at larger places.[7]

The deliberate examination of affiliation helps to answer questions like "Do we address student learning at the departmental or division level?" or "Should we convene a general education assessment design committee that encompasses faculty from affiliated disciplines or with varied backgrounds?" Affiliation isn't the only way to conceive of how faculty work can be best accomplished, but it can provide a way to begin.

The Painful Luxury of Time

Tuning takes years. Patience in philosophy and practice is crucial throughout the work of improving teaching and learning with faculty. There is research that suggests movement on assessment of student learning is usually motivated by accreditation concerns.[8] However, it is unreasonable to expect that work of this type—improving student learning and assessing what students know and are able to do—can be done quickly.

Certainly, steps can be taken quickly and assertively, but to measure results of change, to use those measurements to suggest course corrections, to make those corrections, and to convene those central to measurement and improvement simply takes time. So, in planning to do this work, you must allow for reasonable amounts of time. And you must advise faculty of their timelines for completing tasks and assignments. This alleviates pressure on the faculty working groups, sets a reasonable tone that encourages the right kind of deliberations, allows for measured change and thoughtful consideration of data, and allows the rest of the institution to keep up with changes in terms of support services and policy needs.

Shaping the Message

Patience with this kind of work has its limits, of course. Wise folks have suggested that faculty are tired of the learning outcomes conversation. Right or wrong, faculty feel they have been asked to create student learning outcomes over and over in the last couple of decades, for a variety of reasons, and they would be quick to say that nothing has been done with those outcomes. Yet, despite this fatigue, higher education remains in a landscape that is informed by student learning outcomes only in some places.

In order to reengage the faculty who would claim this fatigue, or to bring to the table those faculty who don't have firsthand experience with this fatigue but have been well-schooled in it by their more senior colleagues, announcing that the department or campus is about to do some work on student learning outcomes may not bring the desired enthusiasm from the faculty.

However, there are many ways to unlock the learning outcomes conversation, and to move toward the assessments that should accompany the outcomes. This is not advocacy of deception, but the acknowledgment that there are many kinds of learning-oriented work to be done on a campus or in a system, so choosing one of those specific areas may be a more enticing charge for faculty than the broad work of developing learning outcomes without context.

For example, particularly given the many different kinds of students who enroll at community colleges, work in prior learning assessment might be a solid first step. As adults and students with military training and experience look to attain a credential, two-year institutions have been challenged to provide academic credit for their acquired knowledge and skills. In order to provide appropriate credit, the experience of the student must be lined up against the courses offered at the college.

Students may use a credit "crosswalk," like the ones developed at Ivy Tech Community College, for previously attained credentials or military experience, or they may take exams offered by departments or third parties, or they may create a portfolio of work to demonstrate competency in one or more courses.[9] However, in order for any of these to function effectively, and for the experience to translate to courses, course-level outcomes are required. And faculty can be called upon to develop or enhance these outcomes.

Additionally, prior learning assessment can be a back-door argument for the need to move to competencies, as described in the second chapter. In considering assessment of prior learning, the need to translate experience and knowledge to traditional courses complicates matters considerably and ends up forcing a square academic peg into a round administrative hole. Instead, it would be better to align already attained competencies from work and military experience with competencies offered as curriculum by the community college as a more efficient and appropriate approach. Close examination of the current state of assessing prior learning reinforces the need for higher education to move aggressively to the language of competencies.

The work of faculty developing student learning outcomes that equate to prior knowledge and skills is a much more exciting and engaging activity than simply launching headlong into the development of student learning outcomes on a course-by-course basis. The end result, however, is the same. In trying to define learning that can be better equated with experience, faculty will have to examine what is core to a course and a program, and how we know that a student has mastered the core knowledge and skills. While the issue of translating prior learning may be resolved, the course, and the students, faculty, and other stakeholders, also benefit from a course that has a much better developed set of student learning outcomes.

All that is left is to align the assessments. This, too, can be done through prior learning assessment work, as a well-developed end-of-course assessment is the perfect instrument to give to a student seeking credit for prior learning. Again the demands of meeting the growing need for credit for prior learning facilitates a more crucial conversation about how to go about measuring skills and knowledge.

Push Back

Messaging student learning outcomes work also includes being prepared to deal with resistance from faculty who see the work of defining and assessing student learning as infringing on their right to deliver curriculum, chosen solely by them, in any way that they choose. There are common myths or assumptions that faculty leap to, sometimes based upon prior experience, other times based on rumor and innuendo, and still others due to assumptions of nefarious intentions on the part of non-faculty stakeholders.

For example, while preparing the Degree Qualifications Profile, considerable effort was put into anticipating faculty concerns and preparing answers that both made the faculty feel listened to and ensured that a consistent, honest message was always delivered.[10] Common misperceptions included:

- Other people are telling me what to teach.
- Developing learning outcomes and assessing against them is the same as "teaching to the test."
- We have done this before and it hasn't made any difference.
- It is bad to "standardize" the curriculum.

Responses to these concerns are context-specific in many cases, but it is important to be prepared to respond. The conversation should not be allowed to devolve into an argument, which is where work like this often gets stalled.

With or Against Faculty

Treating faculty as if they are the enemy in the enterprise of improving teaching and learning, which seems to be the implicit assumption in some places when work gets underway, certainly gets things off to a poor start. Although it can be massaged through the smart use of language—referred to earlier in this chapter—improving teaching begins with a critique of current practice. Imagine how anyone might react if someone arrived at their office and suggested, even subtly, that the reason for the visit was that they were not doing the job well enough and something needed to change. Read cynically, that is what faculty may hear at the beginning of this process. And that is a message that must be avoided at all costs, as it sets faculty on the defensive from the beginning.

Data is often a good, neutral, and relatively safe entry point for these conversations, as it points to areas of weaknesses and keeps the conversation at an academic distance. Confronting faculty with the idea that they must improve their teaching so student learning will improve is more overtly threatening than sharing some test scores or survey data that opens the conversation about student learning and how it might be enhanced. Using the Collegiate Assessment of Academic Proficiency (CAAP) scores on critical thinking, or an employer survey on oral and written communication to suggest curricular review, are more effective and less provocative entry points to the conversation and strategizing.

Here, too, is where the need for faculty champions arises. With some prominent faculty leaders responding to the challenge with good attitudes and genuine interest in improving learning outcomes, other faculty will feel less singled out or targeted. The work becomes a group effort. Carol Geary Schneider, president of the Association of American Colleges and Universities, observed, while drafting the Degree Qualifications Profile, what was really at stake for faculty was a transition from "my work to our work."

From My Work to My Institution

Schneider's words truly capture what needs to be done, and describe the ways our institutions must evolve. Where once it was okay for faculty members down the hall from each other to deliver learning on unrelated subjects without concern for how those subjects might be related, this is no longer acceptable or productive. Because the current population of students has substantially changed from that of a few decades ago, the way in which we approach a curriculum must evolve. Students need a clear road map that suggests how courses are interrelated and add to the whole of a certificate or degree. In particular, at community colleges, where students are often challenged to afford higher education and are looking at workforce opportunities when choosing a program of study, there must be clarity for them about how courses add up to create credentials, and there must be a purposeful approach among faculty when planning courses of study and designing curriculum.

How often have community colleges lost a student who enters the institution declaring themselves as pre-engineering and who finds their first semester schedule to be comprised of English composition, remedial mathematics, a college success course, and an introductory psychology course? From a student perspective, it is easy to see how they might say, "Where is the engineering I was expecting to study?" and how they might quickly lose interest when they encounter challenges.

Where higher education has failed, and where Schneider's "my work" fails us, is that we have not explained to the student, and more importantly, to ourselves, how English, math, psychology, and college success serve individually and collectively to prepare an individual to become an engineer. In essence, "our work" requires that we have these conversations, connect how curriculum works together to prepare students, and then tell the student in a clear and compelling way about how good engineers must write to describe their work plans and needs, use math to address problems, understand psychology in order to combine design with usability and to interact with clients and coworkers. Likewise, we must find ways to convey the importance of being a good student so that they can demonstrate the requisite skills required to receive a degree.

A true move from "my work to our work" requires that we consider the curriculum as a whole and not as a sum of parts and, again, tell this story to our students. Clarity of purpose and understanding the composition of a credential sets students on the right path and eliminates the question of "why this course?" However, only faculty can truly address this issue, and it should be central to their conversations about twenty-first-century teaching and learning.

The Challenge of Adjunct Faculty

Given the changing nature of the higher education workforce, engaging adjunct faculty may be the most crucial element of a faculty engagement strategy. Adjunct faculty are often difficult to connect with due to their loose connection to the institution, the potential that the adjunct role represents only a part-time job to them, the possibility that they are teaching at multiple institutions, and the transient nature of their positions, all of which makes training and engagement encounters necessarily brief and intermittent.

Here is another place where full-time faculty can have a profound impact and should be quickly engaged. Planning to assist adjuncts represents another opportunity to put a fresh spin on developing and assessing student learning outcomes. Returning to the earlier point of understanding affiliation, if adjunct faculty come with particular professional dispositions—particular fields of experience or professional positions—these dispositions can be leveraged by engaging the full-time faculty in puzzling through the best ways to reach and impact the adjunct groups.

There is no better way to consider how to work with adjunct faculty from the world of business than by asking current, full-time faculty who came from the world of business to the community college, for example. Where to place key information, how to frame it for consumption, and how to offer adjuncts a sense of campus culture and priorities are all good topics for a group of full-time faculty and, coincidentally, also lead to full-time faculty debating key issues of curriculum and practice, a conversation we all appreciate taking place.

The work of adjunct faculty can be best supported by adhering to the principles articulated earlier in this book: a focus on student learning, assessing learning, and behaving boldly in developing new approaches to learning. Well-designed and articulated student learning outcomes, and the attendant assessments, give adjunct faculty a sense of the purpose of a course and a fuller understanding of how that course resides in and among other courses required for the certificate or degree.

If full-time faculty prove difficult to engage, directly, on the allegedly tired issue of developing student learning outcomes, or effective assessment of student learning, perhaps they would be more motivated by the notion of conveying their values and culture to adjuncts in order to ensure fidelity to the core concepts of a program. Clear learning outcomes and good assessment practices will convey values and culture.

Assessment of Student Learning Outcomes

No conversation about improving student learning and success can be complete without discussing assessments, and no assessment conversation can be complete without a plan to engage faculty in designing and using those assessments. With K-12 education leaning more and more heavily on standardized testing as evidence of student learning, and with the looming presence of CAAP, the Collegiate Learning Assessment (CLA), the ETS Proficiency Profile, and the like at the postsecondary level, faculty are already acutely aware of an assessment landscape that feels largely out of their control. They are asked to teach to the outcomes described by these instruments, but they are not directly consulted on whether or not these instruments actually address something of worth for their classrooms.

If faculty cannot be easily engaged in working with defining learning, another approach might be to ask them to work with the assessment of learning. Student learning will inevitably come up in assessment conversations, allowing assessment design to serve as something of a back door to the development of learning outcomes.

This is the approach under way at Ivy Tech Community College in Indiana. With a vast and complex system of one college with dozens of campuses and delivery sites, and a combination of state and local control, the Ivy Tech system can best be described as a franchise model. Some things are adhered to by all, but others vary from campus to campus. This may serve students well when it comes to support mechanisms, but it is less appropriate when it comes to the content of courses. After all, when Ivy Tech students seek to transfer to a four-year institution, or return to higher education after a tour of duty in the armed forces, the institution at which they enroll does not distinguish between campuses in the Ivy Tech system.

All the receiving institution knows is that the student took college algebra at Ivy Tech. They assume it means the same thing on every campus in the Ivy Tech system. Common course outlines are intended to assure that comparability, but the college itself needed to move to a more compelling assurance, a common assessment of learning.

As assessment committees at Ivy Tech convened and dug in, they started with assessment design. What sort of instrument should be used to measure learning? It is an easy and safe place to start. But there is no avoiding the fundamental question that comes soon after the design question stalls. What, exactly, are we measuring? And then the real conversation about the essence of a course or field begins. Beginning with assessment, in this case, still led to a thoughtful consideration of the curriculum, of the essence of a credential.

The work at Ivy Tech continues. Addressing the equality of courses has great value for transferring students and prompts discussions among faculty around the essential learning in a course. Meanwhile, this work will invariably expand into assessing general education and program-level outcomes. The beauty of the course-level approach is in building both faculty champions who understand the value of good assessment practices and a campus culture that begins to value assessment in a more substantial way. Both outcomes pave the way for future work in assessment that is crucial to student success.

Diverse Disciplines Lending Their Philosophies

Ivy Tech Community College has also proven to be a good experimental site for another strategy on engaging faculty through assisting other faculty in the work of developing student learning outcomes. Unlike colleagues at the four-year institutions, community and technical colleges have in their midst a set of disciplines that have already mastered the development of outcomes to produce the kind of graduates they wish to have.

The "technical disciplines," as they are sometimes called, including health professions and engineering technologies programs, have long been accustomed to identifying specific knowledge and skills that are crucial to the field, checking with employers to make sure their notions are correct, designing curriculum to teach mastery of these skills and knowledge, and then measuring to ensure that the skills and knowledge have been assimilated.

In fact, in many of these fields, students must pass third-party certification exams to receive credentials or licenses that are every bit as important to their professional life as the certificate or diploma the college awards. Community and technical colleges are fortunate to have faculty accustomed to this approach right down the hall from biology, sociology, and English faculty, who may need some encouragement and role-modeling to think of their disciplines in a similar fashion.

Faculty in the liberal arts will immediately resist the idea that the study of art history can be approached in the same fashion as preparation for design technology. After all, faculty might say, we are teaching students to appreciate and critique works of art, so what can our students demonstrate for us that is comparable to wiring a circuit board or writing code?

This perspective is shortsighted and plain wrong. There are things that would be expected for an art history student to know and be able to do—very clear and specific things. While those skills and knowledge may not include the use of a soldering iron or a voltmeter, they may include the use of a library or a magnifying glass. And both disciplines certainly require some fundamental knowledge, whether it is periods of art history and brush techniques, or ohms and current. Once it can be made clear that without foundational skills and knowledge no discipline can truly be defined and exist, the opportunity for liberal arts faculty to learn from health and technology faculty, and the role these faculty can play in helping other faculty to see their disciplines in a different light, is obvious.

What may prove more challenging is the level of nuance required in good assessment of learning in two vastly different fields. Faculty in construction can quite literally look over the shoulder of a student as they attach a joist or use a plumb bob. Faculty in human services will find it more challenging to ascertain skills and learning while looking over the shoulder of a student reading their text or working with a client.

Naturally, the assessments will be different. In this case, human services faculty will need to develop opportunities to measure knowledge and proficiency, and then rubrics to assess the performance of students. But the work still derives from a clear understanding of what a student should leave a class or program of study knowing and prepared to do. And our technology faculty have been doing that work for more than half a century.

Some fields bridge the gap between the theoretical and the practical. Health sciences, including nursing, are a nice amalgam of practical, performance-oriented tasks and a way of thinking and knowing that informs completing those tasks. In these fields, the work of translating technical knowledge and skills to the realm of student learning outcomes has already been done. Faculty in these fields would also serve as a nice bridge between the more traditional disciplines and fields already well accustomed to thinking about describing and assessing learning in this way.

A PLAN FOR ENGAGING FACULTY

Based on the discussion in this chapter about bringing faculty into a new or refreshed conversation about defining student learning, a plan for how to proceed with this critical work is offered here. That plan might look something like this:

1. Convene a faculty team in the given field, division, or campus, based upon what you know will best suit their identity. Include experienced and inexperienced faculty, those interested in the learning outcomes conversation and not, and sprinkle in some adjuncts. Limit administrators to a facilitating/convening role.
2. Using well-crafted language, charge them to reconsider student learning outcomes in their field or at the general education level (or both) to address any number of issues. Prior learning assessment, new assessment design for assurance of learning,

compatibility with employer needs, or the simple, cyclical need to fine-tune the curriculum all are excellent motivators and do not have to begin with "we need you to develop a list of learning outcomes."

3. Propose a process that includes consulting currently established outcomes; those prescribed by accreditors and professional bodies; feedback from employers, graduates, receiving institutions, and those faculty not privileged to be participating in the conversation. Give the faculty team license to use the feedback they gather and receive it in any way that they choose.

4. Provide the faculty team time to do the work. Set a timeline and check in on progress, but think in terms of months and years, not days and weeks. Provide the means to have periodic face-to-face meetings of the faculty team. Deliberations may be delicate or even provocative, so this work is best done in the same room as much as possible.

5. When the team produces outcomes, invite them to look at the attendant assessments to make sure they are aligned. If they are not, work should begin, similarly configured as the learning outcomes work, to revise or create assessments.

6. Harvest the leadership that emerges from the faculty team to reach out to other teams, serving as consultants or facilitators.

7. Arrange the culture of the department, division, or campus so that the review of outcomes and assessments is a regularly occurring event.

Not all of these strategies will be appropriate for every campus or faculty, but many of them, used in thoughtful planning and preparation, will ease the discussion from one of pain and protest to one of productivity and prosperity. Returning to the first assertion in this chapter, if we intend to truly address learning, not just at the margins, but at the heart of the institution, faculty are the only solution. And the strategies and observations noted here mark a change in the role of faculty on our campuses.

It is no longer sufficient to arrive, hold some office hours, spill forth knowledge about a topic, administer some exams, and call it a day. Instead, faculty need to clearly define learning, build a community of both full-time and adjunct players, collaborate across disciplines to ensure a directed and effective learning experience, assess what is most crucial for student learning, and continue to rise to the challenge of improving student learning and success. Our current challenges are not the fault of faculty, but they cannot be adequately addressed without them.

NOTES

1. Hart Research Associates, "It Takes More Than a Major: Employer Priorities for College Learning and Student Success," paper presented to the Association of American Colleges and Universities, Washington, D.C., April 10, 2013.

2. Richard Arum and Josipa Roska, *Academically Adrift: Limited Learning on College Campuses* (Chicago: University of Chicago Press, 2010).

3. "Read the Standards," Common Core State Standards Initiative, accessed October 28, 2014, http://www.corestandards.org/read-the-standards/.

4. Scott Jaschik, "The Campaign and Higher Ed," *Inside Higher Education,* January 16, 2012, accessed February 17, 2015, https://www.insidehighered.com/news/2012/01/16/presidential-race-brings-scrutiny-candidates-higher-education.

5. Institute for Evidence-Based Change, "Tuning American Higher Education: The Process," accessed October 22, 2014, http://www.tuninguse.org/Library/Newsletters-(1).aspx.

6. Ibid.

7. Lumina Foundation, "Degree Qualifications Profile," accessed October 22, 2014, http://degreeprofile.org/read-the-dqp/appendix-f/.

8. George Kuh and Stanley Ikenberry, *More Than You Think, Less Than We Need: Learning Outcomes Assessment in American Higher Education* (Urbana, IL: University of Illinois and Indiana University, 2009).

9. Ivy Tech Community College, "Credit for Prior Learning," accessed October 22, 2014, http://www.ivytech.edu/pla/.

10. Lumina Foundation, "Degree Qualifications Profile," accessed October 22, 2014, http://degreeprofile.org/read-the-dqp/appendix-f/.

EPILOGUE

Marcus Kolb and Samuel Cargile

The changes proposed in this book represent a quantum leap forward for the learning orientation and student-centeredness for many community colleges. With a focus on student needs and student learning, through innovative curriculum design and delivery, assessment of learning, and faculty engagement, we can be better assured that students will learn what is required to either gain employment or transfer to continue their education. They will persist. They will complete their studies and gain the target credential. Our proposed changes foresee nothing but positives for students.

For the institution, however, the proposed changes represent significant challenges. As discussed, faculty will need to rethink teaching, abandoning the traditional relationship between time and learning. They will have to be more intentional with assessment design and application. They will be required to serve students beyond the traditional teacher/learner relationship. And administrators will need to facilitate these conversations, creating time and space for debate while pushing faculty along to accomplish these transitions to create a more equitable and accessible institution.

This book has described the largely academic evolution our schools and colleges must undergo, but all elements of the institution will need to evolve to support the academic changes. Even if the conversations, led by faculty and focused on improving student learning, go smoothly, parallel work in transforming other elements of the institution to support the renewed focus on learning are necessary.

For example, departing from the credit hour, as a competency-based education (CBE) approach suggests, requires all sorts of supports and processes. CBE requires a new way for students to pay for their learning, detached from the credit hour cost model. How should students be billed for their institutionally sponsored activities if the time to complete a "course" (an antiquated term in the context of competencies, perhaps?) varies from student to student?

Inevitably, as the institution develops a new business model, the role of financial aid in that model also comes into question. Are grants and loans now dependent on the number of competencies a student aspires to master, or do students pay for a fixed period of access to faculty, courses, and support mechanisms, completing as many competencies as time will allow them?

Once students are able to engage in learning at the evolved institution, and it has developed a way to make the new model of teaching and learning cost-effective, recording student skills and knowledge—currently the role of the academic transcript—also becomes a new challenge. And a new version of the academic transcript would be of great value to students.

Current transcripts, typically, record course names and numbers, as well as grades. However, the title of a course does not capture the learning that occurs in a course with much specificity, and the grade that was earned in a course says only the minimum about what the student actually learned. A new transcript, capturing learning in terms of competencies, and expressing student success in terms of competencies attained, would be far more useful for students marketing themselves to employers or their next academic institution. But this transcript needs to be built. And the office of the registrar in our institutions will need to lead the charge in building this new, improved academic record.

Indeed, the very role of faculty must be reimagined along with the academic and process pieces of the institution, if the suggestions in this book are to be fully realized. For the most part, community college faculty already reflect this evolved notion of faculty, with teaching as their primary role (four-year institutions will also need to further evolve their faculty, disaggregating and assigning priority to research and teaching roles). Some versions of the competency-based education model suggest that faculty are coaches first and subject matter experts second, only applying their academic expertise when students are stuck on a particular concept or when competencies are to be assessed.

First and foremost, faculty must point students toward resources that will promote their development of competence. In this role, they are no longer fountains of knowledge, which we can already accept in the face of all of the information democracy that technology has made readily available to everyone. Instead of offering content, faculty become curators of content, tour guides of information. And this fundamental shift in job responsibilities will surely change both the composition of the faculty and the way their jobs are defined and compensated.

Still another aspect of institutions that must change in the face of the evolution of teaching and learning is in recruiting and admissions. With student learning more aligned with workforce needs, assessed at multiple levels, and assured by new models of accreditation, higher education will no longer be the extended-stay *way station* that currently dominates delivery. Rather, it will become more of an Amazon-type educational resource, robust in terms of selection, and highly customized not only to meet, but to anticipate individual wants and needs throughout the life cycle.

Students will come for chunks of learning, centered on specific skills that are in demand in the workplace or that are required to move to the next credential. Freed of the constraints of credits, learning can become even more bite-sized, and learning can be consumed as a series of snacks, only when one needs sustenance, instead of the feast or glutfest that our current certificates and degrees typically impose. Recruiting will become highly focused on finding students with specific skill gaps, and admission will be more focused on assessing what a student can already do as opposed to production of credentials and transcripts. Taking a single course or module, or spending a weekend on an issue, will become the accepted way to amass expertise.

Among many other additional administrative changes also will be the very infrastructure of the campus. Bricks and mortar will always be appealing to a certain subset of the college-going population, particularly the more affluent. There will always be a market for students who wish to participate in the true residential campus experience, complete with learning communities, dining services, athletic events, and social structures.

However, even more of postsecondary education will continue its migration online, and the need for physical space will continue to diminish. Institutional resources will instead be directed toward capacity-building for students to participate meaningfully in learning experiences in the virtual environment. Whether purchasing new, more advanced servers or hiring the information technology staff required to maintain them, the truly forward-thinking institutions will embrace the future of learning rather than continue to try to beautify the existing, outdated model.

It is difficult to envision that disciplines like nursing or teaching could ever be effectively taught and assessed online, but it was once difficult to imagine that any discipline could be handled in this way. Higher education has, begrudgingly in some cases, come to accept this delivery method, and we can anticipate it continuing to assume a more and more significant position in the new models of teaching, learning, and assessment.

The chapters in this book describe an institutional transformation driven by academic evolution. This epilogue describes parts of *a process* evolution. We believe that the academic evolution is the place to start, but an argument can certainly be made that the evolution could begin with processes, which then create the space and opportunity required to transform the academics.

Indeed, some of the resistance encountered in pressing for changes in student learning comes from antiquated processes that can't account for the kind of learning described in this book. We prefer to think that changes in teaching and learning will drag the rest of the institution to the necessary processes, but the ideal model might be for both sides to evolve together.

Is this too much change, too many moving parts? Perhaps. But the increasing—and accelerating—diversity of the students who are coming to our community colleges demand that we *urgently begin this work now*, either together or separately, beginning with the academic or process sides, to maximize their chances for success in our twenty-first-century global economy and community.

INDEX

ABOUT THE AUTHORS

Samuel D. Cargile is vice president and senior adviser to the CEO at Lumina Foundation. He is one of the architects of Achieving the Dream: Community Colleges Count and led its successful transition to an independent nonprofit organization working with more than two hundred colleges to help more students attain a postsecondary degree or certificate. Dr. Cargile holds a Ph.D. in Urban Education with concentrations in Educational Psychology and Sociology from the University of Wisconsin–Milwaukee. He has served as a program officer at the Wallace Foundation and Lilly Endowment, where he developed and managed programs in secondary and higher education that focused on increasing the performance of administrators, teachers and faculty, and students. A significant portion of this work also focused on strengthening the nation's historically black colleges and universities.

Laurie Dodge is vice chancellor of institutional assessment and planning and vice provost for Brandman University, a part of the Chapman University System. She is responsible for undergraduate and graduate degree program outcomes, academic policy, curriculum processes, and development of new programs. Her expertise includes course-embedded assessment, rubric development, faculty engagement, competency-based education, and advancing institutional assessment through the use of technology. She is chair of the Competency-Based Education Network (C-BEN), an invited collaborative group of thirty institutions and four public systems across the nation working together to address shared challenges to designing, developing, and scaling competency-based degree programs. She has served on congressional briefings on the CBE and conducts national workshops on design, assessment, and teaching and learning for competency-based education. Dr. Dodge holds a Ph.D. in School Psychology from Ball State University.

Nassim Ebrahimi is the director for learning outcomes assessment at Anne Arundel Community College and chief executive officer of Ebrahimi Consulting, Inc. She provides leadership and support for the design, implementation, and reporting on the assessment of student learning outcomes at the course, program, and institutional levels. She also assists community colleges across the nation in customizing, systematizing, and improving their assessment processes to further enhance student learning. Dr. Ebrahimi holds a Ph.D. in Psychology from The Pennsylvania State University.

Marcus M. Kolb is assistant vice president for assessment and academic policy at Ivy Tech Community College in Indiana. He plans and manages assessment strategies for student learning and creates and interprets academic policy for the Ivy Tech System of twenty-three campuses and more than 150,000 students. Dr. Kolb holds a Ph.D. in Higher Education from the University of Arizona. Prior to his current position, he served as a strategy officer at Lumina Foundation. His portfolio focused on student learning outcomes and quality in higher education. In this role, he provided leadership for the development and testing of the Foundation's *Degree Qualifications Profile* (2011) and Tuning USA.

Lynn E. Priddy is provost and chief academic officer of National American University, assuming that role in 2013 after fourteen years with the Higher Learning Commission of the North Central Association of Colleges and Schools, the nation's largest regional accreditor. While at the Commission, she served as vice president for accreditation services with responsibilities for accreditation processes, including institutional change and decision processes, peer review, education and training, accreditation demonstration projects, and the Academies for Assessment of Student Learning and Student Persistence and Completion, for which she was the founding director. At National American University, Dr. Priddy oversees all aspects of the educational enterprise, including associate, baccalaureate, master's, and doctoral degrees; she previously served as vice president, director of assessment, and English faculty at Nicolet Area Technical College. She consults nationally and internationally on institutional quality, assessment of student learning, excellence in curricula and pedagogy, and organizational innovation and change. Dr. Priddy holds a Ph.D. in Higher Education, Research, and Evaluation from Capella University.

Jason Wood is president of Southwest Wisconsin Technical College. Before joining SWTC he served as executive vice president for student and academic services at Central Wyoming College, where he provided oversight of all of the college's day-to-day operations as well as leadership for development of new programs and services. In addition, the governor also appointed him to serve as a representative on Wyoming's Complete College America team. Dr. Wood holds a Ph.D. from the Community College Leadership Program at Oregon State University.